PAULA McINTYRE'S
Down to Earth Cookbook

Recipes using great local produce

Dedicated with much love to my Dad, Davy, who says he taught me everything he knows about cooking and for my Mum, Rae, who actually did.

To the memory of

My Uncle Johnny Cochrane – one of life's true gentlemen and a lovely, intelligent man.
Frances McKeague – I miss your warmth, silliness and generosity of spirit every day.
David Semple – a true advocate of Slow Food, an amazing baker, passionate food advocate and great human being.

Published 2015 by Colourpoint Books
an imprint of Colourpoint Creative Ltd
Colourpoint House, Jubilee Business Park
21 Jubilee Road, Newtownards, BT23 4YH
Tel: 028 9182 6339
Fax: 028 9182 1900
E-mail: sales@colourpoint.co.uk
Web: www.colourpoint.co.uk

First Edition
First Impression

Copyright © Colourpoint Books, 2015
Text © Paula McIntyre, 2015

Photographs by David Pauley, The Studio Photography

All rights reserved. No part of this publication may be reproduced,
stored in a retrieval system or transmitted in any form or by any means, electronic,
mechanical, photocopying, scanning, recording or otherwise, without the prior
written permission of the copyright owners and publisher of this book.

The author has asserted his right under the Copyright,
Designs and Patents Act, 1988, to be identified as author of this work.

A catalogue record for this book is available from the British Library.

Designed by April Sky Design, Newtownards
Tel: 028 9182 7195
Web: www.aprilsky.co.uk

Printed by GPS Colour Graphics Ltd, Belfast

ISBN 978-1-78073-096-7

Contents

Acknowledgements 10
Introduction 12

CHAPTER ONE

Vegetables 15

Leek gratin with crunchy thyme and soda bread crumbs 17
Shredded beetroot salad with cumin and ginger 19
Paper bag baked carrots with lemon oil, fennel and chilli, and mint labneh 20
Meat and potato pie 22
Nora's pot roast cabbage 23
Cider braised turnip with crispy bacon 25
Roast pumpkin with ricotta, chilli and mint 26
Onions and tomatoes baked with goat's cheese and lovage 29
Dauphinoise potatoes 30
Scallion and potato pancakes with grilled scallions, crispy bacon and creamy parsley dressing 31

CHAPTER TWO

Fruit 35

Blackcurrant Barbados cream 37
Pavlova with candied strawberries, raspberries and rose petal syrup 38
Christmas pudding 40
Buttermilk cream with poached rhubarb and lavender shortcake 41
Blackberry and pear crumble 45
Apple sponge and homemade cider custard 46
Damson cheesecakes 48
Apple and cider pudding 50
Gooseberry shortcake with elderflower (jelly and cream) 51

Paula McIntyre's Down to Earth Cookbook

Contents

CHAPTER THREE

Meat and Poultry — 55

Daube of beef with beetroot and horseradish 56
Pot roast collar of bacon with split peas and parsley 58
Two roast chickens, three recipes 59
Roast chicken, creamy gravy, sausage stuffing balls and Nicola's bread sauce 60
Chicken broth with potato and soup celery 63
Chicken and broccoli bake 64
Slow roast shoulder of lamb with honey and ale brine, and thyme roast carrots 65
Brisket of beef, Kansas barbecue style 67
Duck prosciutto with apple, celery and walnut salad, and blue cheese dressing 68
Grilled lamb rump steak with mint, chilli and almond butter 70

CHAPTER FOUR

Fish — 73

Glenarm salmon tarator with roast and pickled carrot salad 75
Devilled eggs with smoked salmon 79
Salted ling brandade with guanciale and smoked local butter 80
Cider glazed eels with apple and dulse butter, crystallised dulse, and apple and soup celery dressing 81
Dollaghan or brown trout almondine 85
Smoked salmon fishcakes with horseradish and smoked black pepper dressing 86
Lough Neagh pollan with mealie crushie 87

CHAPTER FIVE

Bread — 89

Pancakes 90
Walnut bread with salted grapes and rosemary 93
Rousel bread 94
Wheaten bread 95
Treacle soda farls 96
Yoghurt flatbread with gorse flowers and black pepper 99
Soda bread with onions, cheese and scallions 100
Pretzel rolls 101

Paula McIntyre's Down to Earth Cookbook

CHAPTER SIX

Sweets and Treats — 103

My Aunt Doreen's Chinese chews 104
Doreen's oat biscuits with whiskey soaked raisins 106
Gluten free carrot cake with cinnamon icing 107
Chocolate truffles 109
Rocky road 110
Buttermilk cake 113
Elderflower poached rhubarb 114
Homemade mincemeat pies 115
Raspberry and hazelnut Madeleines 117
Honeycomb 118
Coffee and walnut cake with white chocolate buttercream 119

CHAPTER SEVEN

Preservation — 123

Sloe and apple Jelly 124
Elderberry capers 125
Elderflower cordial 126
Rose petal syrup 128
Blackberry wine 129
Whin bush and hibiscus Champagne 131
Aunt Emily's raspberry jelly 132
Damson vodka 133
Fermented salsa 134
Magilligan carrot wine 137
Pickled wild garlic buds 138
Plum gin 139

Useful food links 140
Index 141

Acknowledgements

I want to thank all the small artisan producers in Northern Ireland, for your sparkling energy, passion, innovation and drive that has really put this country in the culinary global spotlight. There are too many to mention personally but you know who you are and I appreciate everything you do.

Thanks to my parents Davy and Rae for always being there.

To my wee brother David for all you do and being the only person who can make me laugh until I cry.

To my sister-in-law, Dorothy for friendship and support.

To my nephew Andrew McIntyre for great humour and all your help.

To my niece Rachel McIntyre for your fantastic sense of humour, brilliant baking skills, elderberry picking and our nights with TLC!

And to my aunt Doreen Cochrane for being my baking mentor and sharing all your recipes over the years.

Thanks to Malcolm Johnston, Jacky Hawkes, Rachel Irwin and the team at Colourpoint Books.

To Michele Shirlow, Sharon Machala and the team at Food NI for all your guidance, support and friendship.

To Howard Hastings, Joanne Harvey and the team at Hastings Hotel for a mutual understanding of the food culture here, and your kindness and support over the years.

To David Pauley and Cheryl Johnson of the The Studio in Belfast for the photography in this book and for your good humour, dedication and generosity. I've learned so much from you both.

To Slow Food UK for opening up a wealth of wonderful food opportunities for me.

To BBC NI, especially John Toal and the team, for 10 years of laughter on a Saturday morning.

To Pat McAleer and Newbridge Silver for your generously donated props and support.

To Sam Russell-Morelli for friendship and foodie support.

To Rosanna Morelli and La Lola, Portstewart for ensuring I always have a nice scarf, bag and for some brilliant nights of nonsense.

To Jane McAuley for helping to keep me sane in my teaching career!

To *Farming Life* editor Ruth Rodgers for allowing me to share stories and recipes every week.

Thanks to Anne Marie McAleese for everything you do and unofficial editing!

To Nicola Reihill for a lifetime of friendship and 'getting me'.

To Nicole Morelli for friendship and free lemon sorbet!

And to James O'Connor – my American family.

Thanks to Frank and Linda McCooke of Slemish Market Garden in Ballymena and Patrick Frew of the Happiness Project in Cloughmills for allowing us to use your facilities for the photography and for your wonderful good humour and enthusiasm.

Introduction

My first and last foray into growing vegetables, at the age of 7, was not a success. My grandfather had given me garlic seeds, which I planted and nurtured and then Lupin, our Alsatian dog, ate the white flowers and bulb heads, resulting in our beloved family pet smelling like something that should be added to spaghetti bolognese! She constantly smelled of garlic. Other people had problems with rabbits or pigeons eating their crop, mine came from a four legged hound.

When I first started to cook in professional kitchens, 30 years ago, the emphasis was on importing exotic vegetables. Local carrots, turnips and even potatoes were cast aside in favour of vegetables like baby sweetcorn, and uniformly shaped mangetout and green beans. Fortuitously when I opened a restaurant in Manchester in the early nineties, a friendly taxi driver who also owned an allotment provided me with around half of the fruit and vegetables used on the menus. As a professional chef this was when I really understood the sheer joy of eating locally and seasonally. In autumn he would provide winter greens, potatoes, pumpkins and squashes, and in summer a vast array of tomatoes, beans, peppers, lettuces and corn would arrive, alongside rhubarb, soft summer fruits and plums. It made economic sense and the beautiful produce was like organic paint for a blank culinary canvas.

Thankfully as cooks we now know that working this way makes sense for the economy and the environment. Carbon footprints and waste management are as vital to professional chefs as menu planning and purchasing is. The Italian founder of the Slow Food movement, Carlo Petrini, once said "a gastronome who is not an environmentalist is stupid".

There has also been a sea change in the way we look at animal husbandry, fishing and baking. Everything comes full circle and we now celebrate ancient rare breeds, sustainable lesser known fish and traditional bread making methods. The need for something exotic has all but evaporated and the desire to show off our culinary heritage has never been so pronounced. Far off fields could never be as green and fertile as our own.

Moving back to Northern Ireland from England in 1997, the food scene here was all but non existent. When BBC Radio Ulster gave me my own food series 'McIntyre Magic' back in 2000 there was only a scattering of producers. The first person I ever interviewed on one of the programmes was Walter Ewing, who has a third generation fish shop on the Shankill Road in Belfast. These days he exports his smoked salmon to Dubai, London and New York. Eighteen years ago there were no cheesemakers, butter makers, oil producers, artisan butchers or sour dough bakers and it was a treasure hunt to find artisan producers, farmers who diversified and growers. The restaurant scene struggled in the troubles. With few tourists there was no need to show off our local produce.

Now we have a first class market in St George's in Belfast, with new smaller ones starting all the time, a burgeoning brewing and distilling industry, and new products appearing weekly.

I've been lucky to have been able to showcase food from Northern Ireland to a wider global audience. What I've learned is that food from here is synonymous with quality. Indigenous Northern Irish food is name checked on menus across the rest of the UK, Europe and beyond. Nothing makes me prouder than showing off our produce at home and abroad.

This cookbook is a celebration of Ulster food, with simple recipes dedicated to our culinary legacy. A wise man once said, life is very simple but we complicate it. This philosophy should be applied to the preparation and cooking of food – keep it down to earth and you'll not go wrong.

My notion is for this book be used, smudged, ripped and spilt over at every available opportunity that involves food, family and friends!

Happy Cooking!

CHAPTER ONE

Vegetables

The French have an ethos they call *terroir* (from the Latin *terre* meaning earth), which roughly translated means 'a sense of place in relation to the growing of food'. This has a particular resonance in Northern Ireland. The assumption is that it's a place that is wet, rainy and naturally the land with it, but in fact, the contrast here is as acute as any other larger region. The area around Magilligan in County Derry is reclaimed land from the sea, making for sandy soil that's ideal for growing carrots. A carrot that's been rooted here will taste completely different from one grown in County Down – not necessarily better but they are distinctly different.

Having been brought up in Aghadowey, a lush, flat and slightly boggy area between Ballymoney and Coleraine, potatoes are in my DNA. Alongside Comber, this part of the world is renowned for producing spuds. While Comber enjoys a coastal micro-climate with dry, sloped fields and little frost, Aghadowey is wet, flat and prone to icy nights. Both produce brilliant tubers but they're like day and night in both flavour and texture profiles.

The undulating slopes around the Strangford Peninsula also provide the perfect growing ground for leeks and scallions. The hilly land is naturally irrigated and I love to drive past and see the inky, green stems swaying in the light sea breeze. It remains an unsolved mystery why some chefs serve expensive asparagus in winter when they have these intensely tasty green vegetables right on our doorstep, at a fraction of the price and a multiplicity of the taste.

But what's great about growers here now is that they're experimenting and realising that there is a vast array of vegetables that can be successfully cultivated in this country. Years ago we imported nearly everything but these days people like Robin Cherry from outside Ballymena is producing large amounts of Chinese vegetables, including pak choy. He first started growing them for the Asian community and when I saw them in a specialist supermarket on the Ormeau Road in Belfast, I assumed they'd been flown in from Hong Kong. In reality, they're grown in a football pitch sized poly-tunnel in the naturally undulating landscape above Glarryford in the heart of County Antrim.

A few miles up the road, Frank McCooke runs Slemish Market Garden in Ballymena and grows a beautiful, diverse range of plants. His place is flanked by banks of lovage, popular especially with the Lithuanian community.

When I first started cooking professionally, nearly 30 years ago, chefs imported nearly everything, apart from the most basic vegetables. Now it's ironic in the extreme to think that we import fresh herbs since they grow and flourish so readily here. Visit St George's market in Belfast on any weekend and witness the seasons change as deep purple beetroots, turnips, celeriac, carrots and winter greens are replaced by fennel, tomatillos, courgettes, marrows and heritage tomatoes.

Around Comber in County Down, at certain times of the year you'll see the purple, sunburnt heads of turnips pushing through the soil with their lush, green tops. The bitter heads, normally used for animal feed are, in fact, great fried in butter themselves. A friend of mine in Italy moved to Ireland in the 1960s and really missed the rapini or turnip top vegetable from her native soil. One day they snuck into a local farmer's field and cut some of the green tops from the roots. A curious farmer soon arrived and when they offered a creative explanation, saying it was to feed their animals, he was pacified enough to let them carry on. They were too mortified to admit the truth! Turnips have a bad press – they have an image of being a peasant food but nothing could be further from the truth. Sweet and peppery, tossed in butter, they're a delicious vegetable that should be celebrated at every opportunity when they're in season.

Quality, local vegetables don't need to be pummelled, tortured into intricate shapes or overly spiced. There's no point in gilding the lily.

The recipes in this chapter are a celebration of our *terroir* and I'm letting the vegetables radiate their individual qualities with the help of a few local ingredients, fresh herbs and the odd nod of spicing.

Leek gratin with crunchy thyme and soda bread crumbs

Leeks are the Cinderella of the vegetable world – gently plodding away, often overlooked, with their sparkling beauty largely unnoticed. We favour gaudy alternatives like baby sweetcorn and insipid green peppers. Leeks melted slowly in butter is a delicious way to eat them but to elevate leeks to another level I like to lightly poach and then scorch them on a hot grill pan or barbecue. These are great on their own but for an added dimension pour in a dollop of cream and top with toasty, herby buttery soda crumbs.

INGREDIENTS

- 750g leeks
- 1 vegetable stock cube
- 2 tablespoons local rapeseed oil
- 200ml cream
- ½ teaspoon ground nutmeg
- 2 teaspoons chopped fresh thyme leaves
- 50g butter
- handful chopped parsley
- 100g soda farl

METHOD

- Cut the leeks in half, separating the white from the green.
- Cut the white in half lengthwise through the root, wash well and place in a saucepan. Cover with water and add the stock cube. Simmer gently until cooked through. Remove from the water and pat dry on kitchen paper.
- Split the green of the leek, wash well and slice. Heat a tablespoon of the oil in a saucepan, add the green leeks, season with salt and cook gently for about 15 minutes until soft. Add the cream, thyme and nutmeg, and bring to the boil before pouring into a baking dish.
- Heat a grill pan until smoking hot. Brush the white of the leeks with the remaining oil and place on the pan. Cook for 30 seconds. Slice each piece in 4 and discard the root. Arrange on top of the green leeks.
- Melt the butter and mix in with the soda crumbs and parsley.
- Scatter the mix over the top of the leeks and bake in a 180°C oven for 15 minutes.
- Serve hot as an accompaniment to grilled or roast meats, or on its own with bread.

Paula McIntyre's Down to Earth Cookbook
vegetables

Shredded beetroot salad with cumin and ginger

18

Shredded beetroot salad with cumin and ginger

Up until a couple of years ago the thought of eating beetroot was not one I relished. I found it too earthy, a touch metallic and sharp with vinegar but a visit to Shu restaurant on Belfast's Lisburn Road changed my mind completely. Chef Brian McCann served a goat's cheese salad with shavings of local beetroot. The taste of raw, lightly dressed beetroot was a revelation. It was sweet and packed with flavour.

A plate of local heirloom beetroot, sliced, is like American abstract artist, Jackson Pollock, painting with splashes of yellow, vibrant purple and candy stripes.

This recipe was developed using healthy ingredients such as ginger and turmeric, the addition of some lightly fried onions and a splash of some Burren Balsamics blackcurrant vinegar. It's great as an accompaniment and keeps really well in the fridge. A sneaky spoonful always makes me feel virtuous!

INGREDIENTS

- 2 large beetroots
- 2 tablespoons local rapeseed oil
- 2 red onions, peeled and finely sliced
- 50g grated root ginger
- 2 teaspoons cumin seeds
- 1 teaspoon turmeric
- 1 dessertspoon honey
- 50ml Burren Balsamics blackcurrant vinegar
- salt and fresh ground pepper to taste

METHOD

- Peel and coarsely grate the beetroots. I peel the beetroots and place them in a plastic bag to grate – it means you don't dye yourself and the kitchen walls purple!
- Place in a bowl.
- Heat the oil in a frying pan, add the onions and ginger, and cook until nearly caramelised.
- Add the cumin seeds and the turmeric, and cook for 30 seconds.
- Add the honey and the vinegar and cook for 2 minutes.
- Mix into the beetroot well and season to taste.

Paper bag baked carrots with lemon oil, fennel and chilli, and mint labneh

Seeing a poodle with some of its curly coat shaved off and dyed pink has the same effect on me as seeing a pre-packed bag of carrots, bleached and stripped of their goodness.

Carrots should be caked in muck with their green fronds lush and flowing. Carrot tops are a great indicator of freshness and also make an interesting addition to salad leaves. Carrots belong to the same family as the coriander herb and are natural bedfellows with Eastern flavours because of this connection.

This recipe is for carrots, baked in a parchment paper bag with the addition of a little crushed fennel seed. Fennel seed adds a warm aniseed spice and sweetness. A lick of lemon oil and a hint of chilli makes this a great side dish. The addition of labneh (a strained yoghurt, here with added fresh mint) adds a creamy depth.

Paper bag baked carrots with fennel and chilli

INGREDIENTS
- 4 medium carrots
- 2 tablespoons lemon or regular rapeseed oil
- 1 teaspoon chopped fresh red chilli
- 1 teaspoon crushed fennel seed. Put them in a plastic bag and whack with a rolling pin.
- ½ teaspoon salt

METHOD
- Set the oven to 180°C.
- Peel the carrots and cut off the tops. Wash and pat the tops dry and add to the salad leaves.
- Cut the carrots in half lengthwise and place in a bowl. Add the oil, chilli, fennel seed and salt, and toss well.
- Take a sheet of parchment, approximately 40cm squared. Place the carrots on one half and fold over the paper.
- Start at an end and gather up into a parcel, sealing the edges well.
- Place on a baking tray and bake for about 30 minutes. Have a press on the outside to feel if carrots are soft – if you pierce the bag it'll let out the heat and flavour.
- Bring the bag to the table and slice it open to serve.

Mint labneh

INGREDIENTS
- 500ml local natural yoghurt
- handful chopped fresh mint leaves
- 1 teaspoon salt
- freshly ground black pepper

METHOD
- Take a bowl and place a sieve over it.
- Place a sheet of muslin in the sieve and pour in the yoghurt.
- Leave to strain in the fridge overnight.
- Take the thick yoghurt from top and mix in the mint.
- Salt and pepper to taste.

Paula McIntyre's Down to Earth Cookbook
vegetables

Paper bag baked carrots with lemon oil, fennel and chilli, and mint labneh

Paula McIntyre's Down to Earth Cookbook
vegetables

Meat and potato pie

My natural inclination for cooking potatoes is to steam or boil them in their jackets and toss them in butter, allowing the natural flavour to shine. Meat and potatoes are, however, a match made in heaven and the way to any Ulsterman's heart! This recipe is for meat and potato pie – something I loved to eat when living in the north of England. There they opted for stewing steak, but I've substituted this with good quality mince. The pie crust has the addition of potatoes, which actually makes it a bit lighter and then there's some potatoes cooked with the mince. A hearty, comforting dish that's satisfying on its own; serve with some pickles or open a can of beans to really put a smile on your face!

Pie crust

INGREDIENTS

- 1 onion, peeled and finely chopped
- 2 tablespoons rapeseed oil
- 375g plain flour
- 75g cold butter, diced
- 250g cold mashed potato
- cold water to bind

METHOD

- Fry the onion in one tablespoon of the oil until golden and soft.
- Cool.
- Rub the flour and butter together until the mixture resembles fine crumbs. Mix in the onion mixture, mashed potato and the remaining tablespoon of oil.
- Add about 2 tablespoons of cold water to bind.
- Wrap in cling film and chill.

Meat and potato filling

INGREDIENTS

- 25g butter
- 1 tablespoon rapeseed oil
- 2 sticks celery cut into 1cm dice
- 2 small onions, peeled and chopped
- 750g good quality mince steak
- 1 tablespoon tomato puree
- 200ml beef stock, made with 1 cube
- 1 tablespoon Worcestershire sauce
- 3 tablespoons brown sauce
- 300g peeled potatoes, cut into 2cm dice

METHOD

- Heat the butter and oil in a large pan and add the celery and the onion.
- Cook on a medium heat for about 10 minutes until golden and soft.
- Add the meat and seal off well with the vegetables.
- Add the tomato puree and cook for 30 seconds.
- Add the stock, Worcestershire sauce and brown sauce.
- Place a lid on top and gently simmer until the potatoes are soft.
- Cool.

Nora's pot roast cabbage

Is there anything with a worse image problem than cabbage? I'm of a generation where we were served dried, overcooked cabbage at school and the lingering smelly sock odour still haunts my nightmares!

A curly green cabbage should be treated with respect. Shredding it finely and quickly, before cooking with bacon and butter is a good way to avoid the flatulent smelling gases!

My lifelong friend Nora Scott, originally from Dundalk, and one of the best cooks I know, used to cut a cabbage into wedges and pack it into a big cast iron pot with onion, herbs and stock. This is what converted my 10 year old self into a cabbage lover and it's still my preferred way to get the most out of this much maligned but essentially gorgeous vegetable.

I've taken the liberty of adding some crumbled sausage to the mix but that, of course, is optional.

INGREDIENTS

- 1 medium savoy cabbage
- 1 tablespoon rapeseed oil
- 4 good quality pork sausages, cut into bite size pieces
- 2 onions, peeled and chopped
- 25g butter
- 150ml chicken stock, made with 1 cube
- 1 teaspoon chopped fresh thyme leaves
- handful chopped parsley

METHOD

- Set the oven to 180°C.
- Remove any blemished outer leaves from the cabbage and discard.
- Cut the cabbage in half through the root.
- Cut each half into 3 wedges, through the root.
- Trim off the root at the end but keep it so the wedges will remain intact.
- Heat the oil in a heat proof casserole dish and add the sausages. Cook to seal off well.
- Add the onions and butter, and cook for 2 minutes before packing the cabbage in on top.
- Pour over the stock, add the thyme and season with cracked black pepper.
- Put a lid on the dish and cook in the oven for about 45 minutes or until the cabbage is fork tender.
- Scatter over the parsley and serve.

Paula McIntyre's Down to Earth Cookbook
vegetables

Cider braised turnip with crispy bacon

Cider braised turnip with crispy bacon

Call me shallow but I tend to judge people on their feelings about turnips! They're an emotive vegetable that some people just don't get. A steaming pan of turnip, plunged into crispy bacon with onion, butter and a few grinds of fresh black pepper is in my top 5 favourite dishes. My treat tea when I was growing up was always butcher's beef sausages, turnip and mash. It reminds me of home, my mum Rae and my late Granny Kathleen – food with soul can and should do that.

Turnip and cider are natural culinary bedfellows and this recipe is for turnip braised with cider and topped with crispy bacon. The sweet turnip is lightly cooked with onion and thyme in butter first, then cooked slowly with cider and stock. The bacon adds a crisp texture and salty note.

INGREDIENTS

- 1 tablespoon rapeseed oil
- 25g butter
- 1 medium turnip, peeled, quartered and cut into 2cm dice
- 2 small onions, peeled and chopped
- few sprigs fresh thyme
- 200ml chicken stock
- 250ml local cider
- fresh ground pepper to taste
- 6 rashers streaky bacon
- handful chopped parsley

METHOD

- Heat the oil and butter in a casserole pot over medium heat and add the turnip.
- Cook until starting to colour and add the thyme and onions.
- Cook until the onions are golden and add the stock and cider.
- Cover with a lid and gently simmer for about 30 minutes until the turnips are soft.
- Meanwhile place the bacon on a baking tray and cook in a 180°C oven until crisp. Pat dry and chop.
- Remove the lid and boil to reduce the liquid to sauce coating consistency.
- Season with black pepper, toss in the parsley and scatter over the bacon.

Roast pumpkin with ricotta, chilli and mint

One of the most memorable images etched in my mind is that of a vast array of plump pumpkins at Frank McCook's Slemish Market Garden, in Ballymena, a few autumns ago. They were grown by his American daughter-in-law Lori. There was every shape, colour and size imaginable from grey and blue hued crown prince, to dark green acorn squash and turban shaped onion squash, alongside a gathering of Cinderella carriages.

There were also ears of corn, wrapped in their creamy husks, behind the regimental lines of colourful gourds. It was like a scene from New England but they were all grown on Antrim soil.

One of my favourite restaurants is Osteria del Tempo Perso in the village of Casalveri, in the Lazio region of Italy. It's run by two brothers Marco and Matteo and their mamma Sabrina. Everything they serve is delicious but the way they serve simple roast pumpkin at room temperature, with nothing added except a little oil, is sublime. I've added my take with some ricotta cheese (recipe included if you fancy having a go at making it), chilli and mint but the essential thing is a great sweet Ulster pumpkin to start with!

Roast pumpkin

INGREDIENTS

- 1 small culinary pumpkin – crown prince is my favourite
- 2 tablespoons rapeseed oil
- seasalt
- 1 red chilli
- 150g good ricotta cheese
- handful fresh mint leaves
- juice 1 lemon

METHOD

- Set the oven to 200°C.
- Cut the pumpkin into 6 wedges.
- Remove the seeds, wash them and pat dry on kitchen paper.
- Toss the pumpkin and chilli in the oil and set on a baking tray. Scatter with seasalt and place in the oven.
- Spread the pumpkin seeds on a tray lined with parchment paper and place in the oven.
- Remove the chilli after 10 minutes. Cool, peel, deseed, chop and set aside.
- Remove the seeds from the oven when they start to pop (after about 20 minutes).
- Remove the pumpkin when it's soft and coloured a little.
- Place the pumpkin on a platter and scatter over the ricotta.
- Chop the pumpkin seeds coarsely, and add the mint and chilli. Mix in the lemon juice and a little bit more oil if you wish.
- Drizzle over the pumpkin and serve.

Homemade ricotta cheese

INGREDIENTS

- 600ml whole milk
- 300ml double cream
- 1 teaspoon salt
- 3 tablespoons vinegar

METHOD

- Place the milk, cream and salt in a non-reactive saucepan and simmer.
- Add the vinegar and cook, stirring until the mixture curdles.
- Pour into a sieve lined with 2 layers of muslin
- Cool and transfer to the fridge.
- After a few hours, remove the layer of cheese (curds) from the muslin.
- Discard the muslin but the remaining liquid, or whey, can be used as a substitute for buttermilk in breads or scones.

Paula McIntyre's Down to Earth Cookbook

vegetables

Roast pumpkin with ricotta, chilli and mint

Paula McIntyre's Down to Earth Cookbook
vegetables

Onions and tomatoes baked with goat's cheese and lovage

Onions and tomatoes baked with goat's cheese and lovage

Lovage is one of those unique tasting herbs that you can't buy in the supermarkets and have to grow yourself. It's a prolific herb that has the potential to take over a spot in your garden. Mine was coming along nicely until a slug climbed to the top of it, eating every leaf along the way. A morning sprinkle of coffee grounds round the roots keeps the brutes away and it's flourished ever since!

Buying locally grown onions is always the way to go – ideally they'll have a dusting of mud and hard skins. Baking them in foil with salt, oil and the chopped lovage stalks turns them into golden spheres of loveliness.

Layering the golden onions with local tomatoes, dotting with goat's cheese and baking, results in a dish that just needs some homemade bread to soak up the juices.

INGREDIENTS

- 6 small local onions, peeled and halved
- 2 tablespoons rapeseed oil
- handful lovage
- 250g goat's cheese
- 100ml double cream
- 500g local tomatoes
- salt and fresh black pepper

METHOD

- Set the oven to 180°C.
- Take a sheet of foil and brush with oil.
- Place the onions on top, cut side up and drizzle over the oil.
- Pick the leaves from the lovage and set aside.
- Chop the stalks and scatter over the onions, seasoning with a little salt.
- Gather up the foil to seal and place on a tray. Bake for about 45 minutes, until soft.
- Lightly brush a baking dish.
- Mix half the cheese with the cream and season with salt and pepper. Chop half the lovage and add to the mix.
- Slice the tomatoes and layer half in the baking dish. Season with salt and pepper and scatter over the remaining cheese. Top with the rest of the tomatoes and spoon over the cheese and cream mixture.
- Bake in the oven for 20 minutes.
- Scatter over the remaining lovage leaves and serve.
- Lovely on its own with bread or serve with roast beef, lamb or chicken.

Paula McIntyre's Down to Earth Cookbook
vegetables

Dauphinoise potatoes

Potatoes define us as a nation – you're either a waxy or a floury person! I've been cooking this classic French recipe since my days at culinary college and every time I set it on the table it gets a great reaction – like an old friend you're always glad to see. Local potatoes, enrobed in garlic and nutmeg infused cream and baked gently – what's not to love?

INGREDIENTS

- 500g King Edwards or Maris Piper potatoes
- 250ml double cream
- 250ml whole milk
- 1 clove garlic, crushed
- ½ teaspoon fresh grated nutmeg
- salt and pepper

METHOD

- Butter a baking dish.
- Scrub the potatoes clean and slice as thinly as you can.
- Place in cold water.
- Put the cream, milk, garlic and nutmeg in a pan and bring to a simmer.
- Add salt and pepper to taste.
- Allow to infuse for 15 minutes.
- Set the oven to 160°C.
- Drain the potatoes and dry on kitchen paper.
- Layer up in the dish and pour over the cream mixture.
- Bake for about 45 minutes or until a knife inserts easily.
- Serve immediately.

Scallion and potato pancakes with grilled scallions, crispy bacon and creamy parsley dressing

For me you get double for your buck with scallions. The bottom white part is sharp and oniony and the green is bright and zingy. In New Orleans they use the green and chuck the white – a cardinal sin in this book!

This recipe uses the green to flavour a pancake and then the whites are split, rubbed with oil and cooked in a griddle pan. They take on the stripes of the pan and this naturally caramelises them – a win, win situation. The mashed potato in the pancake adds a certain creaminess and is a handy way for using up leftover potato. Crispy bacon adds a crunch and local curly parsley is mixed into a creamy dressing to set the whole thing off.

Scallion and potato pancakes

INGREDIENTS

- 250g mashed potatoes
- 100g self raising flour
- sliced green part of 4 scallions
- ½ teaspoon salt
- 100ml whole milk
- 1 egg
- 25g melted butter
- rapeseed oil for cooking

METHOD

- Mix the potatoes, flour, scallions and salt in a bowl.
- Whisk the milk, egg and butter in a separate bowl and then mix into the potato mixture.
- Set aside for 10 minutes.
- Wipe a medium hot frying pan with rapeseed oil and drop tablespoons of the batter into the pan – don't overcrowd.
- When bubbles appear on the surface of the pancakes, flip them over and cook for a minute on the other side.
- Cool on a wire rack.

Paula McIntyre's Down to Earth Cookbook
vegetables

Grilled scallions

INGREDIENTS

- White part of 4 scallions
- ½ tablespoon rapeseed oil

METHOD

- Heat a griddle pan until hot.
- Split the scallions lengthwise through the root.
- Brush with oil and cook on the pan until marked and wilted.
- Set aside.

Crispy bacon

INGREDIENTS

- 8 rashers smoked dry cure streaky bacon or 8 slices Peter Hannan's guanciale (see recipe on page 88)

METHOD

- Cook gently on a dry pan until crisp.
- Pat on kitchen paper.
- Keep the fat for roasties.

Creamy parsley dressing

INGREDIENTS

- 2 tablespoons cider vinegar
- 1 teaspoon Dijon mustard
- 50ml crème fraîche
- 50ml local rapeseed oil
- handful chopped parsley
- salt and pepper to taste

METHOD

- Put all the ingredients in a jam jar and shake until they come together.

To finish...

- Place the pancakes on a big platter.
- Chop the grilled scallions and scatter on top.
- Chop the bacon and add to each.
- Top with the dressing.

Paula McIntyre's Down to Earth Cookbook
vegetables

Scallion and potato pancakes with grilled scallions, crispy bacon and creamy parsley dressing

CHAPTER TWO

Fruit

Nothing, but nothing, gladdens my heart more than the gift of some seasonally grown fruit. A motley box of dappled, multicoloured apples, fragrant, plump quinces, and inky damsons will set my heart racing and brain working at full tilt debating all the cooking possibilities.

We are blessed, most years, to have a teeming harvest of local treasures, like those appley autumn delights plus scarlet summer strawberries, ravishing red raspberries, regal, ruby rhubarb, buxom blackberries, blingy blackcurrants, gorgeous gooseberries and pert pears.

Because the season is limited, it's best to preserve their delicious elixir by either freezing or making into jams. Freezing is the easiest solution and if, like me, your enthusiasm gets the better of you, it can become a fruit tombola towards the end of the season with each layer offering up a new seasonal surprise!

Armagh apples now have internationally renowned Protected Geographic Interest status (PGI) which confirms their uniqueness, alongside foods like Parma ham, Stilton cheese and Champagne – all only available in these specific areas. Fresh apple tart made from sharp, crisp Armagh Bramleys is in our food DNA. The best examples I've tasted haven't been in restaurants, but in people's homes or at country shows. The annual shows also provide a showcase for the best of other types of baking and jam making. It's wonderful that young people are taking up the gauntlet of this tradition and keeping this sacred Ulster staple alive.

An abundance of wild fruit grows in every county of Northern Ireland. My childhood is brimming with memories of blackberry picking, eating tiny wild strawberries from the side of the road and lip puckering gooseberries from a hedge.

My father's granny grew raspberries in the moss near where we lived at Blackhill in Aghadowey. They're old vines, and hard to locate now, but they have an intensity of flavour that's an unforgettable, mouth watering experience. It's like tasting history. When they reach the end of the season and have endured endless summer rain, a lick of sunshine and time, they exude a flavour that's hard to beat. This applies to any locally grown raspberry but naturally nostalgia may dictate my loyalties.

My parents have a damson tree in an adjoining field. I applied, and failed, for planning permission to build there a couple of times, so the fruit from this tree is probably the most expensive I've ever eaten! It's good to track a tree and remember where you were the previous year at blossom and fruit time. It's a gage of your life. I freeze some of the precious fruit, and make wine or infusions with the rest.

My aunt Doreen gave me a rhubarb plant that had started life on an allotment in Belfast in the 1950s, later the site of Queen's University halls of residence, on the Malone Road. I never stop being mesmerised that the black pile of mush never fails to produce pink shoots once winter makes way for spring. My rhubarb harvest may be small – just a few stalks – but I make the most of them. Rhubarb is an emotive fruit here and, like apples, a pie made from it is a memory of childhood, family and love.

The recipes in this chapter are the ones I go to for comfort and a celebration of fruit. They're all quite indulgent, with no fromage frais or low fat in sight. These are puddings for a Sunday or special occasions with no apologies for decadent additions!

Warm apple sponge and homemade custard, for example, isn't something you're going to have every day but when you do it feels right to give it the deluxe treatment.

Blackcurrant Barbados cream

A few years ago some friends and I formed a book club. It started off very well with books being read and discussed very cerebrally. Before long though it quickly morphed into a bookless, supper club! This is one of the recipes from the book/supper club that was made by my friend Linda. Her daughter was studying in Reunion Island in the Caribbean at the time and while visiting her she picked up an array of vanilla pods, which grow prolifically on the island, at a fraction of the cost that you can buy them for here. It's a simple cream and yoghurt confection with vanilla. She topped it with fresh berries but blackcurrants cooked with sugar make a great accompaniment too.

Barbados cream

INGREDIENTS

- 1 vanilla pod
- 250ml Greek yoghurt
- 250ml double cream
- 4 tablespoons dark muscovado sugar

METHOD

- Split the vanilla pod lengthwise and scrape out the seeds.
- Bury the remaining pod in sugar to make vanilla sugar or dry in a 100°C oven until crisp.
- Cool, blend with 500g of granulated sugar, pass through a sieve and keep in an airtight container.
- Mix the seeds with the yoghurt.
- Lightly whip the cream to soft peaks and fold into the yoghurt.
- Place in 4 bowls, smooth off the top and sprinkle a spoonful of the sugar evenly over each.
- Chill for at least an hour to allow the sugar to permeate through the yoghurt.

Blackcurrant compote

INGREDIENTS

- 250g fresh or frozen blackcurrants
- 75g castor sugar

METHOD

- Place the blackcurrants in a pan and add the sugar.
- Cook gently until the berries just start to burst.
- Cool and spoon on top of the cream.

Pavlova with candied strawberries, raspberries and rose petal syrup

Among the most common questions I get asked is "how do I stop my pavlova from cracking?" My response is to follow the recipe, use older egg whites, and allow it to cool in the oven. If I'm honest I don't mind a bit of cracking – isn't that what cream is for?! I like a crisp on the outside, chewy in the middle meringue as opposed to a big 'soapy' version. Small meringues look prettier than a single big one and they're easier to manage.

Once the pavlova is made, what you put on top is your choice. I have a personal aversion to kiwi fruit but it's your party!

I love strawberries and candying them is a good way of bringing out the natural sweetness. Tart, fresh raspberries provide flavour and texture contrast.

There's a rose in my garden called Reine des Violettes. It's deep purple and has the most glorious, musky fragrance. I managed to capture its scent in a rose petal syrup. You could use your favourite smelling rose – just make sure it hasn't been sprayed with pesticides. Drizzled over pavlova with strawberries and raspberries, and hey presto the essence of summer is on a plate.

Pavlova

INGREDIENTS

- 4 large egg whites, at room temperature
- 150g castor sugar
- 100g icing sugar
- 1 teaspoon cornflour
- 2 teaspoons white wine vinegar
- 250g fresh raspberries
- 250ml whipping cream
- 1 tablespoon of either dried rose petals, nasturtium petals or viola flowers

METHOD

- Older eggs make better meringues so if you've some near the sell by those are ideal.
- Set the oven to 100°C and line a baking sheet with parchment paper – or do two if making mini ones.
- Take a scrupulously clean bowl, add the egg whites and whisk.
- When they've reached stiff peaks, or will hold their shape if the bowl is tipped upside down, add a third of the castor sugar and continue to whisk. When it's incorporated, add another third and then the final increment.
- Whisk for a minute then fold in the icing sugar in 2 batches. Whisk again. Mix the cornflour with the vinegar and add this to the meringue. Whisk for another minute.
- Spoon the meringue into a circle. You can do this free hand or use a pencil to draw a perfect circle. Either way have the meringues roughly the same height for evenness of cooking. If you're doing smaller ones, have them about the same size.
- Bake for an hour, less if you do smaller pavlovas, or until the top is firm and crisp. Turn off the oven and allow them to cool within it.

Candied strawberries

INGREDIENTS

- 500g hulled strawberries, larger ones cut in half
- 100g castor sugar
- 200ml white or rose wine
- zest and juice 1 lemon

METHOD

- Place the sugar in a non stick frying pan over high heat and cook to a golden caramel without stirring too much (it will cause the sugar to crystallise).
- Add the wine, lemon zest and juice, and boil to a thick syrup. This will take about 10 minutes.
- Add the strawberries, toss them in the syrup and remove from the heat.
- Cool.
- Spoon whipped cream onto the pavlova and top with the strawberry mixture. Dot with some fresh raspberries and drizzle over the rose petal syrup. Scatter over some dried rose petals, fresh nasturtium flowers or violas.

Rose petal syrup

INGREDIENTS

- 125g fragrant rose petals (ensure they're from a bush that hasn't been sprayed with pesticides)
- 750g castor sugar
- 350ml water
- 1 lemon, thinly sliced

METHOD

- Wash the rose petals in cold water and pat dry on kitchen paper.
- Place in a bowl with 250g of the sugar and scrunch together to release the scent.
- Cover with cling film and leave overnight, giving it the odd stir.
- Place the remaining 500g of sugar, the water and the lemon in a pan and bring to the boil.
- Simmer until the sugar has dissolved and add the soaked petals and sugar.
- Simmer for 30 minutes or to a syrupy consistency.
- Strain through muslin and pour into sterilised bottles.

To finish...

- Spoon whipped cream onto the pavlova and top with the strawberry mixture.
- Dot with some fresh raspberries and drizzle over the rose petal syrup.
- Scatter over some dried rose petals, fresh nasturtium flowers or violas.

Christmas pudding

Last year I entered this pudding into the Slow Food UK Christmas Pudding challenge and was named runner up. I'm not competitive but was delighted at this, especially as the winner, Tom Aikens, has a two Michelin starred restaurant in Chelsea. I beat Fortnum and Mason and a good collection of award winning chefs and other food emporia.

It's rich and fruity as a good Christmas pudding should be. Serve with whipped cream or the cider custard from the apple sponge recipe on pages 46–47.

INGREDIENTS

- 650g mixed raisins, sultanas and chopped figs
- 150ml dry cider
- 150ml heather ale
- 3 tablespoons quince jelly
- 200g soft butter (at room temperature)
- 200g soft dark brown sugar
- 2 large eggs
- 50g plain flour
- ½ teaspoon baking powder
- 150g breadcrumbs
- 100g grated Armagh Bramley apple
- zest 1 orange
- ¼ teaspoon each ground cinnamon, clove, mixed spice and ginger
- 50ml damson vodka

METHOD

- Place the fruit in a large bowl.
- Whisk the cider, ale and quince jelly together, and pour over the fruit.
- Soak overnight – give it a good stir now and again.
- Beat the butter and sugar until pale and fluffy. It's best to do this with an electric beater and will take at least 10 minutes to achieve.
- Beat in the eggs one at a time.
- Sift the flour and baking powder together, and mix into the butter mixture.
- Add the breadcrumbs, apple, orange zest, spices and damson vodka.
- Stir well, make a wish and spoon into 2 one pound pudding bowls.
- Cover the top with a circle of parchment paper, followed by a loose sheet of tin foil. Tie round the sides with string.
- Steam for about 4½ hours.
- Rest for 10 minutes in the pudding bowl before turning onto a plate before serving.

Buttermilk cream with poached rhubarb and lavender shortcake

Last year I had the honour of cooking this dessert at a dinner given in honour of culinary icon Darina Allen on a rare visit to Northern Ireland. Darina has an international reputation and I was a bit daunted by the task ahead. As it was May, the local rhubarb was already in full swing. The remit was to showcase ingredients from County Down and using Abernethy Butter from Dromara was a good place to start. Will and Alison Abernethy handchurn the butter and sell to great delis and restaurants around the UK. The residual buttermilk from the process is the way proper buttermilk should be – watery in consistency with flecks of gold piercing through the white. For the dinner I turned this into a simple set cream and served it with buttery lavender shortcake sandwiched with Aunt Emily's raspberry jelly (recipe on page 132). The icing on the cake was a dollop of Will Taylor's Glastry Farm raspberry and lavender icecream. All the plates were cleared and thankfully so was Darina's!

Buttermilk cream

INGREDIENTS

- 3 gelatine leaves
- 100ml whole milk
- 120g castor sugar
- 1 vanilla pod
- 375ml buttermilk
- 125ml lightly whipped cream

METHOD

- Soak the gelatine leaves in cold water for 10 minutes.
- Split the vanilla pod in half lengthwise and scrape the seeds into a saucepan.
- Add the pod, milk and sugar, and simmer until the sugar has dissolved. Remove from the heat.
- Squeeze the water from the gelatine and add to the milk mixture.
- Cool and then add the buttermilk.
- Fold in the lightly whipped cream and pour into glasses or serving dishes.
- Chill for at least 4 hours to set.

Poached rhubarb

INGREDIENTS

- 4 medium sticks rhubarb, cut into bite sized sticks
- 125g castor sugar
- 125ml water
- 50ml Grenadine
- splash of liqueur if you wish

METHOD

- Set the oven to 180°C.
- Boil the sugar, water and Grenadine until the sugar has dissolved and the liquid is syrupy.
- Add the liqueur (I like to add some of my own sloe gin, Shortcross Gin from Downpatrick or Cointreau) if using it.
- Pour over the rhubarb and cover with a piece of parchment paper.
- Place in the oven to poach. This will take about 20 minutes but keep checking as it will turn to mush quite quickly.
- Remove from the oven and cool.

When you've taken out the rhubarb and some of the juice for the dessert, the rest of the liquid can be kept for up to a week in a jar in the fridge. It makes a jaunty addition to gin and tonic or a glass of Prosecco!

Lavender shortcake

INGREDIENTS

- 250g plain flour
- 200g cold butter, chopped into 1cm dice
- 100g icing sugar
- 2 egg yolks
- ¼ teaspoon dried and chopped lavender flowers
- about 5 tablespoons raspberry jelly (or substitute jam)

METHOD

- Place the flour, butter and sugar in a bowl, and rub until the mixture resembles fine breadcrumbs. Alternatively pulse in a food processor.
- Add the egg yolks and lavender, and mix to a dough.
- Place on a lightly floured surface.
- Roll to about ½cm, ¼ inch thick. Keep moving the dough around while you roll to stop it sticking.
- Cut into circles using a 3cm, 1½ inch cutter.
- Place on a lightly buttered baking tray and bake for 12–15 minutes or until golden and firm.
- Place on a wire rack to cool.
- If not using immediately, store in an airtight tin.
- Sandwich with the raspberry jelly to serve.

Paula McIntyre's Down to Earth Cookbook

fruit

Buttermilk cream with poached rhubarb and lavender shortcake

Paula McIntyre's Down to Earth Cookbook
fruit

Blackberry and pear crumble

My teenage niece Rachel is a talented, natural baker who can seemingly rustle up a magnificent chocolate cake or scones when there are very few ingredients in the house! She's been making this classic pudding on her own since she was 8 and her variations include traditional apple with cinnamon, plum and orange, rhubarb and strawberry, and pear and raisin. We developed this one together for the book but the topping is her baby!

INGREDIENTS

- 4 pears, peeled, quartered, cored and each quarter cut into 3
- 175g castor sugar
- 100ml water
- ½ teaspoon ground cinnamon
- 300g blackberries (fresh or frozen are both good)

METHOD

- Place the pears in a saucepan and add 75g of the sugar, cinnamon and the water.
- Simmer gently until soft.
- Add the remaining sugar and blackberries, and simmer for 5 minutes.
- Place in a lightly buttered baking dish.

Crumble topping

INGREDIENTS

- 300g plain flour
- 250g butter at room temperature
- 300g castor sugar
- 50g flaked almonds

METHOD

- Set the oven to 180°C.
- Rub the flour and butter together until the mixture resembles coarse crumbs. Mix in the sugar well.
- Spoon over the fruit mixture, scatter over the almonds and bake for 30 minutes or until golden and crisp.
- Serve while still hot with either icecream or custard.

Apple sponge and homemade cider custard

This pudding is also known as Eve's pudding (because it's so tempting!) and is simple, classic and as beautiful as it gets. Armagh Bramley apples have a crisp natural sharpness. When you stew them with sugar and top with a quivering, buttery sponge, you have the makings of a perfect dish. We were all brought up with apple sponge and custard at school but this version calls for a toot of sweet, local cider in the mix, that adds a luxurious, adult tang.

Apple sponge

INGREDIENTS

- 750g Bramley apples, peeled, cored and sliced
- 100g castor sugar
- zest and juice ½ lemon
- 25g butter

METHOD

- Place the apples, sugar, lemon zest and juice, and butter in a saucepan, and cook until they start to soften.
- Place in a buttered baking dish and pack them down well.

Sponge topping

INGREDIENTS

- 175g soft butter
- 175g soft brown sugar
- 3 eggs
- 175g self raising flour
- 1 tablespoon milk to loosen
- 1 teaspoon vanilla extract

METHOD

- Set the oven to 180°C.
- Beat the butter and sugar until pale and fluffy – this will take 10 minutes using an electric mixer.
- Add the eggs 1 at a time and then fold in the flour and vanilla.
- Spread over the top of the apple mixture.
- Bake for 45 minutes or until golden and an inserted skewer comes out clean.

Homemade cider custard

Substitute milk for the cider if you wish.

INGREDIENTS

- 150ml local sweet cider
- 200ml whipping cream
- 6 egg yolks
- 75g castor sugar
- 2 tablespoons cornflour

METHOD

- Place the cider and cream in a saucepan and heat until just scalded – not boiling.
- Whisk the egg yolks, sugar and cornflour in a bowl for 1 minute.
- Pour over half of the hot cream mixture and whisk well.
- Pour this back into the remaining mixture in the pan.
- On a low heat, stir constantly until the mixture coats the back of a spoon – be careful – there's a dangerpoint between silky custard and scrambled eggs!
- Serve immediately or it will keep in a thermos flask for an hour.

Damson cheesecakes

Florence Irwin, otherwise known as the 'cookin woman', was a broadcaster and cookery writer from County Down who did much to document food from this part of the world in her books, work with RTE and in her weekly column in the *Northern Whig* newspaper. The stories in her book *The Cookin Woman* are great and the recipes surprisingly innovative for the time – the beginning to middle of the last century. One of her recipes is for hot apple cheesecakes, a familiar traybake using a pastry base, stewed apples and then baked with a almond and egg white topping. I've had these over the years but always served cold, as an accompaniment to a cup of tea. Served straight from the oven they're a revelation! I've replaced the apple with damson jam but any jam would work well. They're delicious with the cider custard in the recipe on page 47.

Shortcrust pastry

INGREDIENTS

- 150g plain flour
- 100g cold butter
- 50g castor sugar
- 1 egg yolk
- cold water to bind

METHOD

- Rub the flour and butter until the mixture resembles fine crumbs (you could do this in a food processor).
- Add the sugar and mix well.
- Make a well and add the egg yolk and a tablespoon of cold water and mix well. Add a little more water if necessary to make a dough.
- Wrap in cling film and chill for 10 minutes.
- Butter a 12 hole baking tray.
- Roll the pastry out to about ¼cm. Cut out circles and press into the holes.
- Add a teaspoon of damson or your favourite jam to the bottom of each cheesecake.
- Set the oven to 180°C.

Cheesecake topping

INGREDIENTS

- 2 large egg whites
- 50g almonds
- 75g castor sugar
- 25g rice flour
- ¼ teaspoon baking powder

METHOD

- Whisk the eggs to stiff peaks and fold in the almonds and sugar.
- Beat for 3 minutes then whisk in the rice flour and baking powder.
- Spoon onto the jam and bake for 15 minutes.
- Cool in the tray for 2 minutes then take out with a knife.
- Serve straight away.

Paula McIntyre's Down to Earth Cookbook

fruit

Damson cheesecakes

Apple and cider pudding

Craft cider making is a burgeoning industry in Northern Ireland. When you have some of the best apples in the world, it makes sense to make this wonderful drink. This is a recipe that celebrates the many culinary facets of the apple – there's cooking apple, eating apple, apple jelly and cider in the mix here. Serve it bubbling from the oven with a big scoop of icecream!

INGREDIENTS

- 75g apple jelly
- 2 large Armagh Bramley apples
- 3 red eating apples
- 125g self raising flour
- 60g butter
- 175g castor sugar
- 275ml dry cider or local apple juice, at room temperature
- 1 teaspoon mixed spice
- ½ teaspoon cinnamon

METHOD

- Set the oven to 190°C.
- Butter a baking dish and spread the jelly over the bottom.
- Peel and core the cooking apples, cut into quarters and then cut each quarter in 3.
- Place onto the jelly.
- Quarter and core the red apples. Cut each quarter in half and scatter around the cooking apples.
- Rub the flour and butter until the mixture resembles fine breadcrumbs.
- Mix in the sugar before whisking in the cider or apple juice to a smooth batter. Whisk in the spices.
- Pour the mixture onto the apples and bake for about 35 minutes or until golden and an inserted skewer comes out clean.
- Serve immediately.

Gooseberry shortcake with elderflower (jelly and cream)

My mum, Rae, has been making this shortcake recipe for years. I also use other recipes, which are included throughout the book, but we refer to this one as 'thee' shortcake. It's easy to rustle up and there's no rolling involved. While it's great sliced and served with a cup of tea, it's impressive as a centre piece dessert with seasonal fruit on top. Gooseberries and elderflowers are serendipitously in season together, in early summer, and are a wonderful match. Crunchy shortcake with zingy, sweet gooseberries, billowy cream and a fragrant elderflower jelly – mother nature at her best.

Shortcake base

INGREDIENTS

- 225g chopped butter
- 250g plain flour
- 115g castor sugar
- 85g cornflour

METHOD

- Set the oven to 170°C and line a baking tray with parchment paper.
- Melt the butter in a saucepan and then remove from then heat.
- Beat in the other ingredients and press into the baking tray. Smooth off the top and make furrows with a fork.
- Bake for about 25 minutes or until golden and firm.
- Allow to cool.

Gooseberry and elderflower compote

INGREDIENTS

- 750g gooseberries
- 100g castor sugar
- 50ml elderflower cordial (shop bought or you can make your own using the recipe on page 126)

METHOD

- Top and tail the gooseberries – I do this with a set of nail scissors I keep exclusively for this purpose!
- Place in a saucepan and add the sugar and cordial.
- Cook gently until the gooseberries start to burst.
- Cool.

Gooseberry cream

INGREDIENTS

- 100ml strained juice from the compote
- 250g mascarpone cheese
- 200ml double cream
- 2 tablespoons icing sugar

METHOD

- Boil the juice to reduce by half.
- Whisk into the mascarpone and then fold in the cream and the icing sugar.

Elderflower jelly

INGREDIENTS

- 3 gelatine leaves
- 250ml local sweet cider
- 50ml elderflower cordial
- 1 tablespoon castor sugar

METHOD

- Soak the gelatine in cold water for 5 minutes.
- Place the cider, cordial and sugar in a pan, and simmer until the sugar has dissolved.
- Remove from the heat.
- Squeeze the water out of the gelatine leaves and add to the hot liquid.
- Place in a lightly oiled and cling film lined tray. For this amount I tend to use a plastic Chinese restaurant takeaway tray, so anything roughly that size.
- Cool the hot liquid and pour in.
- Chill until set.

To finish...

- Spoon the compote onto the shortcake.
- Dice the jelly and dot around.
- Pipe on the elderflower cream.
- Garnish with some fresh elderflowers if available.

Paula McIntyre's Down to Earth Cookbook

fruit

53

Gooseberry shortcake with elderflower (jelly and cream)

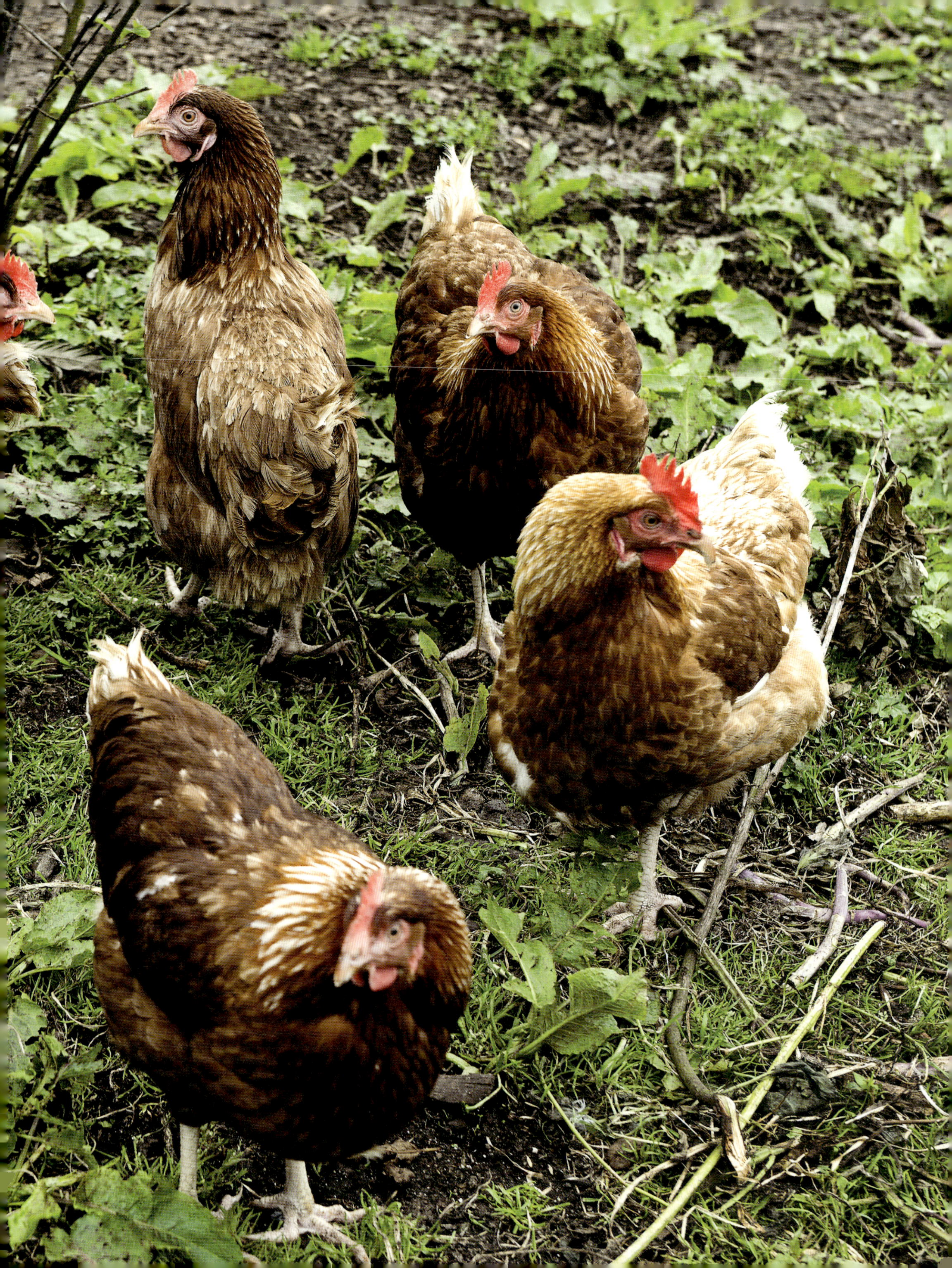

CHAPTER THREE

Meat and Poultry

Lush, fresh pastures, soft rain and good husbandry all contribute to a world class meat industry in Ireland. Our beef and lamb is the envy of the rest of the globe and rightly so. The industry here is still largely based on small family farms with generations of farmers who care passionately about the land and their livestock. Good animal welfare and an attention to traceability are all responsible for this well earned reputation.

With the best will in the world, you can have a great product but it takes a good butcher to bring it to the next level. In this field we are truly blessed with passionate master artisans who have excellent skills and combine vision and imagination to add value to meat.

It's not enough now to just keep the premium cuts like fillet and loin, and mince the rest. Nose to tail eating (or 'rooter to tooter' as my American chef friend Todd Waline likes to call it) isn't a fad. It makes economic sense and the cheap cuts are where the flavour is. Butchers are going back to old fashioned preservation methods like curing, salting and sausage fermentation. Rare breeds like Saddleback and Tamworth Pork, and Longhorn and Moilie beef are now back in the frame.

When it comes to buying poultry – buy the best chicken, duck or turkey you can afford. One really good chicken from a farm you know is better than three cheap ones from an unknown source. Not only will the meat taste infinitely better but the resulting stock and pan juices will be of a fine quality base for soup or gravy.

When you age meat properly you lose on weight, but add to the quality. The price will be higher, but cut down on the portion size and add more vegetables, grains and pulses. It's better for the environment as well as your pocket!

For me a good steak is a real treat. Lightly sprinkled with seasalt, room temperature meat is fired onto a pumping hot pan for a minute each side. While the meat rests, deglaze the pan with a splash of decent red and mount with a little butter – let the natural juices sing.

The recipes in this chapter are ones that I use at home. Contrary to popular myths, you very rarely get served a tasting menu when a professional cook makes dinner in their own house! I love slow cooked, cheaper cuts of meat like collar of bacon, chump steak and shoulder of lamb. The fall apart nature of the meat and the resulting unctuous natural juices are what I want, with great local vegetables to accompany.

The key to good meat sourcing is to find a butcher you trust, like and are able to communicate with – the rest will follow naturally.

Paula McIntyre's Down to Earth Cookbook

meat and poultry

Daube of beef with beetroot and horseradish

People are often intimidated by cooking for professional cooks, for fear they'll critique their food and ridicule them. This couldn't be further from the truth! When you cook for a living you are delighted to have anything prepared for you. Many of the stand out meals of my life have been in family homes where something is plonked in the middle of the table, without ceremony, and everyone digs in. When the lid comes off a casserole dish and the rich aroma of beef exudes, that's a happy time. No need to torture ourselves over individual dressed plates of perfectly cooked steak – leave that to the restaurants.

A well made stew is a good example – well aged meat that has been marinated in red wine and cooked slowly with bacon lardons, onions and some vegetables. When served with a big bowl of mash, you couldn't ask for anything more. The combination of beef with smoky, cured bacon, earthy, sweet beetroot, and hot, peppery horseradish is a joy to the palate.

INGREDIENTS

- 1kg stewing steak, cut into 5cm sized cubes
- 300ml red wine
- 2 carrots, peeled and chopped into 2cm dice
- 1 stick celery, chopped
- 2 onions, peeled and chopped
- few sprigs fresh thyme
- 2 cloves garlic, peeled and crushed
- 4 medium beetroots
- 1 teaspoon fennel seeds
- zest 1 orange
- few grinds black pepper
- 1 teaspoon salt
- 100g chopped streaky smoked bacon
- 1 tablespoon plain flour
- 1 tablespoon tomato puree
- 250ml beef stock
- 1 tablespoon horseradish sauce

METHOD

- Place the steak in a bowl and add the wine, carrots, celery, onions, thyme and garlic. Mix well, cover with cling film and place in fridge overnight.
- Set the oven to 170°C.
- Drain the meat and keep the marinating liquor.
- Remove the meat from the vegetables and pat dry.
- Heat a tablespoon of the remaining oil in a pan until smoking hot and add half the meat.
- Cook until sealed all over and transfer to a casserole dish.
- Repeat with the remaining beef.
- Add the bacon to the pan and cook until crisp.
- Remove from pan and add the reserved vegetables.
- Cook for about 5 minutes or until the onions are golden.
- Add the flour and tomato puree and mix well. Add the reserved marinade and beef stock and stir until the sauce starts to thicken.
- Add to the meat in the casserole, mix it up and then add a lid. Place in the oven for about 2 hours or until fork tender.
- Meanwhile take a sheet of foil and brush with some oil.
- Cut the beetroots in quarters and place on the foil. Sprinkle over the fennel seeds, orange zest, black pepper, 2 tablespoons of oil and the salt.
- Wrap up the foil in a loose parcel and bake for about an hour or until the beetroots are soft.
- Peel the skin, trim them and cut each quarter into 3 and set aside.
- When the meat is tender, add the horseradish and cooked beetroot.
- Cook for another 10 minutes.
- Check seasoning and serve with mash.

Paula McIntyre's Down to Earth Cookbook

meat and poultry

Daube of beef with beetroot and horseradish

Pot roast collar of bacon with split peas and parsley

Collar of bacon seems to be a forgotten cut. Located at the back of the head, it requires long, slow cooking. It's quite a fatty joint but don't be put off by that – after braising gently, douse with honey and roast to render down the fat. Many butchers are, thankfully, curing their own bacon now and if you give them notice I'm sure they'd be delighted to set some of this cheaper part aside for you.

When you add soaked split peas to bacon or ham the result is magical. The peas soak up all the porcine saltiness. A handful of chopped fresh curly parsley at the end of cooking will add a verdant freshness to the whole dish. Serve with potatoes boiled in their jackets and anointed with butter.

INGREDIENTS

- 150g dried peas, soaked in water overnight
- 1kg collar bacon, tied
- 1 tablespoon rapeseed oil
- 2 sticks celery, coarsely chopped
- 2 onions, peeled and quartered
- stalks from a handful bunch of curly parsley, finely chopped (keep the leaves)
- 1 carrot, peeled and coarsely chopped
- 1 bay leaf
- 4 crushed black peppercorns
- 750ml water
- 1 small leek, finely chopped

METHOD

- Set the oven to 160°C
- Heat the oil in a casserole dish and seal the bacon all over until the fat is golden.
- Add the celery, onions, parsley stalks, carrot, bay leaf, peppercorns and water.
- Drain the peas and add to the pot.
- Cover with a lid and place in oven for about 2 hours.
- Add the leeks and cook for a further 20 minutes.
- Remove the bacon and rest for 10 minutes.
- Chop the parsley leaves and add to the vegetable mixture.
- Slice the bacon and serve on top.

Two roast chickens, three recipes

My friend Nicola Reihill always cooks two big chickens at a time. She uses some of it for a traditional roast dinner and then transforms the leftovers the next night into a Moroccan inspired dish or Thai curry. It makes sense when you have the oven on anyway to utilise the energy as much as you can.

A golden, crispy roast chicken with stuffing and gravy can be the most enticing thing to eat. I like to rub the chicken with oil first, crank up the oven and get it nice and golden then lower the heat and baste regularly for the rest of the cooking time. I've had bread sauce in the past and never really warmed to it – it looked like a poultice and tasted of nothing! Nicola makes one that changed my mind – creamy, tasty with a hint of nutmeg.

She also makes a fantastic chicken and broccoli bake. This is one of those timeless classics that we've become a bit sniffy about. The truth of the matter is there is nothing as comforting as chicken, broccoli, a creamy sauce with a hint of curry, topped with a crispy cheesy topping.

When you've cleared the chickens as much as possible, make stock from the carcasses. Simmering them with vegetables and herb stalks makes an ideal base for soup and sauces, and any excess can be stored in the freezer. When I make gnocchi, I bake the potatoes and then I'm left with the skins, which I'm loath to discard. Infused in chicken stock, they slightly thicken it and give it a nutty, roasted taste, which is a perfect base for a chicken and soup celery broth.

Paula McIntyre's Down to Earth Cookbook
meat and poultry

Roast chicken, creamy gravy, sausage stuffing balls and Nicola's bread sauce

We tend to reserve stuffing for our turkeys at Christmas time but really it's too good to have only once a year. It's a good idea to ask your local butcher to keep you some of the meat he uses to make sausages for this.

Roast chicken

INGREDIENTS

- 1 x 1.5kg chicken
- 1 stick celery, chopped
- 1 onion, peeled and quartered
- few sprigs thyme
- 2 tablespoons local rapeseed oil
- 1 teaspoon seasalt

METHOD

- Set the oven to 210°C.
- Place the vegetables and thyme in a roasting tray, and put the chicken on top.
- Rub the oil all over the bird and season with the seasalt.
- Place in the hot oven and cook for 15 minutes.
- Baste with juices and turn the oven down to 150°C. Cook for a further hour, basting occasionally.
- To check if it's done, insert a skewer into the leg and if the juices run clear it's ready.
- Allow to rest, covered, for 10 minutes while you make the gravy.

Creamy gravy

INGREDIENTS

- 1 tablespoon plain flour
- 25g soft butter
- 300ml chicken stock (either fresh or from 1 cube)
- cooking juices and vegetables from the roast chicken

METHOD

- Transfer all the cooking juices and vegetables into a saucepan. If you're inclined you can remove some of the fat but I think the 'schmaltz' adds to the sauce.
- Bring the juices to heat in the pan.
- Mix the flour and butter to a smooth paste, and add to the hot juices and vegetables.
- Whisk to remove lumps and add the stock.
- Bring to the boil and simmer for 5 minutes.
- Blend in a jug blender or with a stick blender.
- Pass through a sieve, check seasoning and serve in a warmed gravy boat.

Sausage stuffing balls

INGREDIENTS

- 1 small onion, peeled and finely chopped
- 25g butter
- 450g good quality sausage meat
- 35g breadcrumbs
- handful chopped parsley
- 1 teaspoon crushed fennel seeds
- few grinds fresh black pepper

METHOD

- Set the oven to 180°C.
- Fry the onion gently in the butter until soft and golden.
- Cool and mix well into the sausage meat with the other ingredients.
- Form into walnut sized balls and place on a lightly oiled baking tray.
- Cook for approximately 25 minutes or until firm.

Bread sauce

INGREDIENTS

- 1 small onion, cut in half
- 1 bay leaf
- 2 cloves
- 500ml whole milk
- ¼ teaspoon freshly grated nutmeg
- 6 peppercorns
- 100g fresh breadcrumbs
- 25g butter
- 2 tablespoons double cream

METHOD

- Place the onion on the bay leaf and stud it with the clove to hold it in place.
- Pour the milk into a pan and add the onion, nutmeg and peppercorns.
- Bring to the boil, turn off and allow to infuse for 2 hours.
- Remove the peppercorns, bay leaf and cloves, and bring back up to heat.
- Blend the onions in the milk, add the breadcrumbs and stir to a smooth sauce.
- Simmer for 15 minutes before whisking in the butter and cream.
- Check the seasoning and serve.

Paula McIntyre's Down to Earth Cookbook
meat and poultry

Chicken broth with potato and soup celery

Soup celery is an indigenous herb to Northern Ireland and forms a vital part of both our traditional broth and in the chicken soup here.

Chicken broth

INGREDIENTS

- 2 baked potatoes
- 1 roasted chicken carcass
- 1 carrot, peeled and cut in half lengthwise
- 3 onions, 1 halved, 2 peeled and finely chopped
- 2 sticks celery, 1 halved and 1 finely chopped
- 100g soup celery, finely shredded
- 25g rapeseed oil
- a few parsley stalks and a handful chopped parsley

METHOD

- Cut the potatoes in half, remove the flesh and set aside.
- Place the carcass in a saucepan and cover with cold water.
- Add the baked potato skins, the carrot, the halved onion, the halved celery stick and the parsley stalks.
- Bring to the boil and simmer for 2 hours.
- Remove the carcass and baked potato remnants, and discard.
- Remove the vegetables, chop and set aside.
- The remaining liquid is the stock for your broth.
- Fry the rest of the onions and the celery in the oil over a medium heat until soft and golden.
- Add the stock and bring to the boil.
- Add the chopped, cooked vegetables.
- Chop the potato into dice and add with the soup celery.
- Simmer for 10 minutes.
- Add the chopped parsley and serve with warm bread.

Paula McIntyre's Down to Earth Cookbook

meat and poultry

Chicken and broccoli bake

Like a classic country and western song, when this recipe is performed well, it's a show stopper.

INGREDIENTS

- 1 x 1.5kg chicken roasted and meat stripped from carcass
- 50g butter
- 1 tablespoon rapeseed oil
- 2 onions, peeled and chopped
- 1 small leek, split lengthwise, washed and chopped
- pinch of salt and 1–2 grinds of fresh black pepper
- 50g plain flour
- 2 teaspoons curry paste
- 450ml chicken stock (either made from the carcass or using 1 cube)
- 350g broccoli
- 2 tablespoons crème fraîche
- 75g breadcrumbs
- 75g grated mature cheddar

METHOD

- Heat the butter and oil in a large pan.
- Add the onions and leek, season with salt and pepper, and cook gently until soft and golden.
- Mix in the flour and curry paste to a smooth paste.
- Add the stock and whisk or stir until all the lumps have gone.
- Simmer gently for 10 minutes.
- Cut the broccoli into florets and finely slice the stumps.
- Cook in boiling salted water for 4 minutes.
- Drain well and add to the onion mixture with the chicken.
- Remove from the heat and stir in the crème fraîche.
- Spoon into a baking dish and sprinkle over the crumbs and cheese.
- Bake in a 180°C oven for about 20 minutes or until golden and bubbling.
- Serve with some boiled potatoes.

Slow roast shoulder of lamb with honey and ale brine, and thyme roast carrots

Brining meat in a salty/sweet solution will not only add flavour and juiciness to your meat but will also help to reduce moisture loss during the cooking process – a 'win win' situation. I also use this brine for pork roasts, chops and chicken. You could substitute cider for the ale (or leave it out and add water).

For me slowly cooked lamb, falling tenderly off the bone, a sweet crust on top, with roast carrots redolent of thyme is a true taste of the perfect Sunday lunch.

Honey and ale brine

INGREDIENTS

- 1.5 litres water
- 350ml local ale
- 6 juniper berries, crushed
- 1 tablespoon crushed black peppercorns
- 250g seasalt
- 100g brown sugar
- 50g honey

METHOD

- Place all the ingredients in a pan, bring to the boil and simmer until the sugar and salt have dissolved. Cool completely.

Shoulder of lamb

INGREDIENTS

- 1.5kg boned and tied lamb shoulder
- 1 litre chicken stock
- few sprigs fresh rosemary
- 2 onions, peeled and quartered
- 500g medium carrots, peeled and cut in half lengthwise
- 2 tablespoons rapeseed oil
- 150ml local ale
- 1 tablespoon honey

METHOD

- Place the lamb in a plastic container and pour the cool brine on top until submerged. Place in the fridge for at least 4 hours or preferably overnight.
- Drain off the brine and pat the lamb dry with kitchen paper.
- Set the oven to 120°C.
- Place the lamb in a casserole pot and add the onions, rosemary, and pour in the stock.
- Cover with a lid or foil and place in the oven for about 5 hours or until the meat falls apart when poked with a fork.
- Crank the oven up to 180°C.
- Toss the carrots in the oil and season with salt.
- Place the lamb in a roasting dish and save the juices for gravy.
- Scatter the carrots around the lamb and return to the oven.
- Meanwhile boil the ale and honey to a syrup.
- After 20 minutes brush some syrup over the lamb and toss the carrots around.
- Repeat frequently until the carrots are cooked and the lamb is golden and glazed – about another 20 minutes.
- Remove from the oven and rest for 10 minutes in a warm place.
- Slice the lamb and serve with the carrots.

Paula McIntyre's Down to Earth Cookbook
meat and poultry

Brisket of beef, Kansas barbecue style

Brisket of beef, Kansas barbecue style

Like New World cooking, Kansas City Barbecue was one of those styles that I was aware of but never actually thought too much about. That changed when I was invited to do demonstrations and cook at Kansas State University and Johnson County Community college in Kansas in the Spring of 2015. One of the chefs at Johnson County, Eddie Adel, was very generous with his recipes and gave me a copy of his own barbecue bible. Barbecue in Kansas and the Southern States of America doesn't mean throwing meat on a grill. Rather it's spiced, smoked 'long and slow', and coated with barbecue sauce for the last stage of cooking. To replicate this at home you could 'kiss' the meat with smoke on your grill at the last minute and glaze with the sauce. Having a smoker is on my culinary bucket list. There's a jar on the kitchen window sill of 20p pieces saving up for this luxury item – last count there was still £985.80 to go!

Brisket of beef

INGREDIENTS

- 2kg boneless brisket
- 3 teaspoons smoked sweet paprika
- 2 teaspoons dried garlic powder
- 2 tablespoons dried onion powder
- 1 teaspoon ground black pepper
- 1 teaspoon English Mustard powder
- ½ teaspoon all spice
- 2 teaspoons seasalt
- 100g Demerara sugar

METHOD

- Mix up all the spices and set half aside for the barbecue sauce.
- Rub the mix all over the beef, cover with cling film and chill overnight.
- Pat the meat dry in the morning and rub all over with oil.
- Set the oven to 220°C and place the meat in a lightly oiled roasting tin.
- When the oven is hot add the meat and cook to seal for 15 minutes.
- Place 250ml of water or ale in the bottom of the tray, cover with foil and lower the heat to 130°C.
- Cook for 3 hours or until fork tender.
- Remove the foil and brush with barbecue sauce.
- Cook for a further half hour, basting 3 times with sauce.
- Rest and slice the meat.
- Serve with the pretzel rolls on page 101 and extra sauce.

Kansas barbecue sauce

INGREDIENTS

- 2 tablespoons local rapeseed oil
- 2 cloves garlic, minced
- 2 tablespoons tomato puree
- remaining spice blend from brisket rub
- 200ml tomato ketchup
- 200ml water
- 100ml white malt vinegar
- 2 tablespoons treacle
- 1 tablespoon Worcestershire sauce

METHOD

- Fry the garlic in the oil until golden and add the tomato puree.
- Cook for 30 seconds then add the remaining ingredients.
- Bring to the boil then simmer gently, stirring frequently, for 30 minutes.

Duck prosciutto with apple, celery and walnut salad, and blue cheese dressing

Duck breasts are now readily available and wonderful paired with a crisp, fresh salad. Curing them prosciutto style adds an extra salty spice dimension to them. Duck and apples are natural bedfellows and crisp celery, warm walnuts and blue cheese completes the taste profile. These days we're blessed with world class artisan blue cheeses and whipping them into a creamy dressing just sets this whole dish off to a tee.

Duck prosciutto

INGREDIENTS

- 2 large duck breasts
- 100g seasalt
- 100g dark brown sugar
- 6 crushed juniper berries
- 2 teaspoons cracked black peppercorns
- 1 teaspoon smoked paprika

METHOD

- Place the duck breasts on a sheet of cling film, flesh side up.
- Mix the salt, sugar, juniper, peppercorn and smoked paprika together, and spoon over the duck, pressing in lightly.
- Wrap tightly in the cling film and chill for 3 days to cure.
- Wash off the cure and pat dry with kitchen paper.
- Place skin side down in a dry pan over low heat and cook for about 10 minutes until the skin is crisp and rendered.
- Flip over and cook for 2 minutes on the other side. Cook for longer if you like it well done.
- Rest then slice thinly, lengthwise.

Apple, celery and walnut salad

INGREDIENTS

- 2 red eating apples
- juice 1 lemon
- 50g walnuts
- 2 sticks celery
- 1 head radicchio lettuce

METHOD

- Quarter the apples, remove the core and slice as thinly as you can. Pile up the slices and cut into sticks.
- Toss in the lemon juice to stop them discolouring.
- Toast the walnuts in a dry pan for 30 seconds and add to the apples.
- Slice the celery as thinly as you can and toss into the apple mixture.
- Cut the radicchio in half and remove the core. Brush with oil and season with salt.
- Place on a hot griddle to scorch.
- Shred and place on a plate.
- Scatter over the shredded duck and spoon round the apple salad.
- Serve the blue cheese dressing on the side.

Blue cheese dressing

INGREDIENTS

- 125g crème fraîche
- 2 teaspoons horseradish sauce
- 2 tablespoons Burren Balsamics apple vinegar
- 100ml local rapeseed oil
- 50g crumbled local blue cheese (Kearney Blue or Young Buck would work beautifully)

METHOD

- Whisk the crème fraîche, horseradish and vinegar together.
- Slowly whisk in the oil and then the cheese.
- Whisk until smooth.
- Season to taste.

Paula McIntyre's Down to Earth Cookbook
meat and poultry

Grilled lamb rump steak with mint, chilli and almond butter

Lamb rump steak

INGREDIENTS

- 4 x 200g lamb rump steaks, fat well trimmed
- 2 tablespoons rapeseed oil
- few sprigs fresh rosemary
- 1 teaspoon seasalt
- pinch sugar
- 2 teaspoons apple vinegar

METHOD

- Place the oil in a bowl, add the salt, rosemary, sugar and vinegar, and mix well.
- Add the lamb and coat well.
- Leave for 20 minutes at room temperature.
- Heat your barbecue or grill pan.
- Place the lamb rump on the grill and seal off for 2 minutes each side.
- Move to a cooler place in the barbecue or lower the heat on the grill pan and cook for a further 8 minutes, turning occasionally.
- Rest for 5 minutes and slice before serving topped with a good slice of the butter.

Mint, chilli and almond butter

Compound butters are an ultra cool way of adding a bit of gusto to grilled meats, poultry or vegetables. It's a classic French method, epitomised by maitre d'hotel butter and involves making a reduction of wine, shallot and acid, and whipping into butter with aromatics.

When I make an infused butter, I produce more than I need and freeze it in portions – it's handier to make a big batch in your blender and great to have them on hand to add a bit of pizzazz to your cooking. On the regular occasions that my fridge has garlic, chilli and herbs that are nearly past their best, I whizz them into a butter to preserve their goodness.

You could experiment by substituting other herbs, red wine or cider instead of white wine and adding other citrus fruits or vinegars. Let rip with your imagination!

INGREDIENTS

- 1 red jalapeno chilli
- 1 teaspoon rapeseed oil
- 1 shallot, peeled and finely chopped
- 200ml dry white wine
- juice 1 lemon
- zest 1 lemon
- 200g butter at room temperature
- 10g picked mint leaves (mint stalks don't work well here)
- 5g chopped parsley
- 50g toasted flaked almonds, chopped coarsely

METHOD

- Brush the red chilli with oil and either hold with tongs and scorch directly on your gas burner or place in a 200°C oven and cook for 10 minutes until scorched.
- Cool, peel and deseed (or keep the seeds in if you like extra heat).
- Boil the shallot, wine and lemon juice in a pan until all the liquid has evaporated.
- Cool.
- Blend the chilli, shallot, reduction, lemon zest and herbs to a smooth paste, and transfer to a bowl.
- Fold in the nuts and then place on a sheet of plastic wrap.
- Roll into a sausage shape and chill.
- Wrap what you don't need into sections and freeze for up to 3 months. It's great with chicken and pork too.

Paula McIntyre's Down to Earth Cookbook

meat and poultry

Grilled lamb rump steak with mint, chilli and almond butter

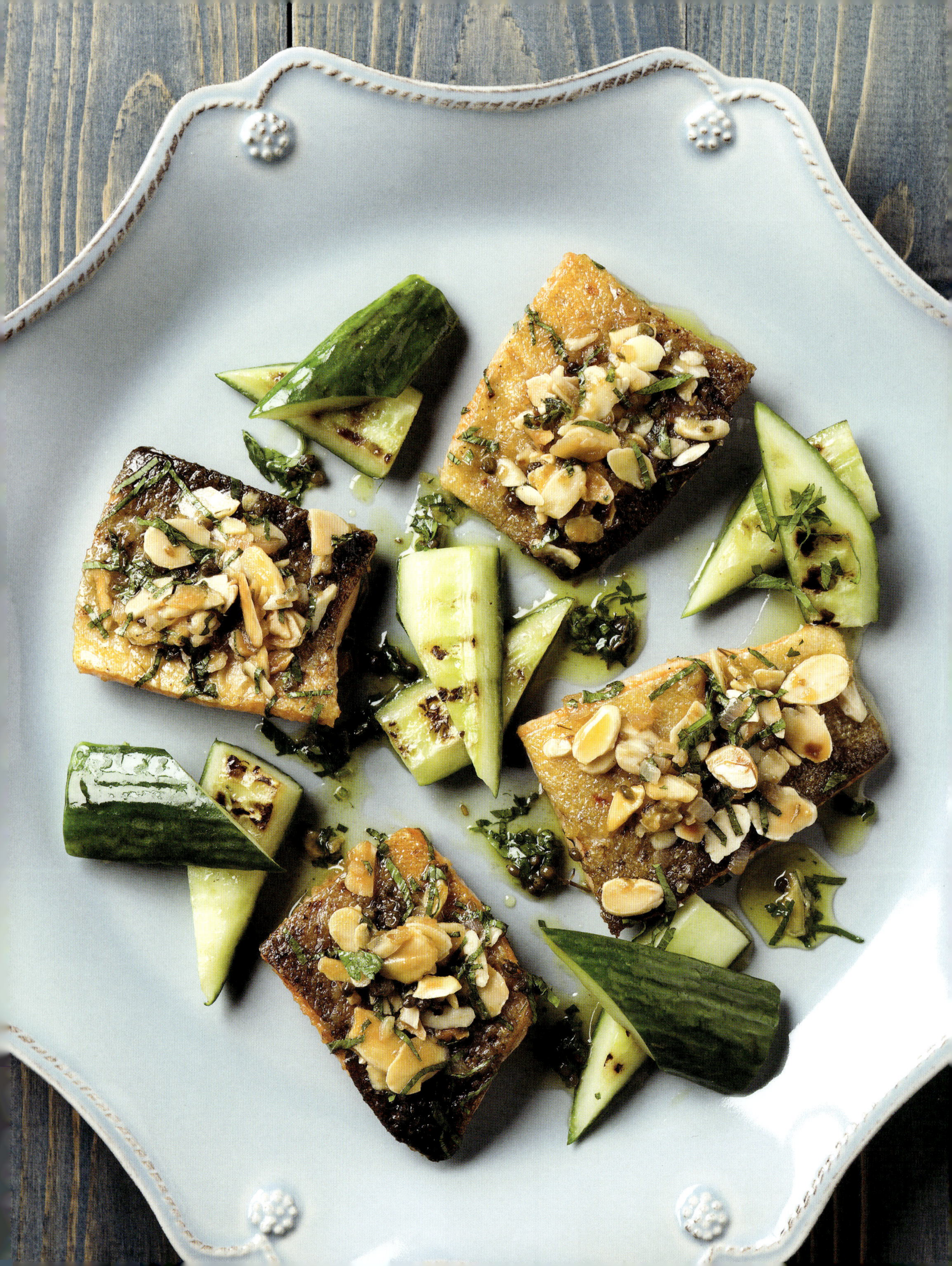

CHAPTER FOUR

Fish

Fish from waters around the coast of Northern Ireland, from Kilkeel and Ardglass in County Down, past Larne to Red Bay in Antrim and on towards the mouth of Lough Foyle in Londonderry, are among the most magnificent in the world and universally celebrated. Our cold, tidal waters make the ideal habitat for lobsters, scallops, langoustines, mussels and oysters. When you eat a lobster in Spain or France, chances are it came via Red Bay in Cushendall or Portavogie in County Down. While we're learning to embrace our local seafish here, we tend to ignore the rich treasures that come from our rivers and loughs. Eel and Pollan from Lough Neagh are mainly exported to Northern Europe, where countries like Holland and Switzerland can't get enough of it. If you've ever eaten traditional jellied eels in London, they most certainly originated in Lough Neagh.

I grew up near the banks of the Agivey river in Aghadowey and took wild salmon for granted. People would turn up at our door with a glistening, sharp beaked, beautiful fish, wrapped in old newspaper. It was duly gutted and frozen for a dinner party, when my mother would poach it in the fish kettle and cover it with cucumber scales – well it was the 1970s!

Pollution has seen salmon numbers dwindle dangerously and now fishing of these prized fish is reserved for rich people with deep pockets. Glenarm Salmon fisheries, located just off the coast near the village after which it's named, is as near to wild salmon as you're likely to get. The fish are stored in nets, a mile out to sea so they have the benefit of currents. They're fed on pellets that are as organically close to what they would eat in the wild, resulting in a brand name check on menus all over the world. Third generation fishmonger Walter Ewing, from the Shankill Road in Belfast, masterfully cold smokes it and his version sells in high end delicatessens in London, New York and Dubai.

My Grandparents lived beside the Ballinderry River, outside Cookstown and my grandfather was a keen fisherman. On hot summer evenings, brown trout and dollaghan would pierce through the water in the mill dam beside their house, to catch flies. The feeling of exhilaration when my brother David or I caught a fish is still a vivid memory for both of us. All children should learn to fish, if only to respect the food nature provides. I can't remember a lot about last week, but I can remember every fish I ever caught like it was yesterday.

As part of a BBC outside broadcast in Draperstown I met a young man called Matthew Doyle. We spent the morning talking about fishing and how he spent most of his spare time on the banks of the Moyola River in County Derry. In the age of X-Boxes and facebook, it was refreshing to see a 17 year old talk so passionately about an age old past time.

These days, if I want a fish I know exactly where to go. My old school friend, Stephanie Holmes, has a lake outside Castlerock, called Moorbrook Lodge. Her farmed fish is really tasty and some even weigh up to 5 pounds. Oily fish like this are best barbecued on a balmy evening with a touch of oil, some lemon and very little else – maybe a glass of Chardonnay!

I adore seafish but with the exception of salmon and ling, this chapter is dedicated to the earthy fish from our loughs, manmade lakes and rivers if you're lucky. We should embrace this indigenous fish more and have it available for the many visitors who flock here every year – it's part of our landscape, history and food culture.

Glenarm salmon tarator with roast and pickled carrot salad

Driving along the Antrim coast road, from Larne, there's an arch through which you can see the village of Glenarm tucked in the corner. Glance to the right and you'll see what looks like giant rubber rings in the middle of the sea. This is Glenarm Organic Salmon Farm and the fish produced here have the benefits of strong tides and a feed that emulates what wild salmon eat. The fish is as near to wild in texture and taste as is possible, and is exported to top restaurants in Ireland, the UK and as far as Dubai.

In Turkish cuisine tarator refers to the inclusion of walnuts. Their slight bitterness works with the oily salmon, warm sumac spice, fresh mint and the zip of pomegranate molasses. I love fish and carrots together. This combination of roast soft orange spears with crunchy pickled ones coaxes them to show off their many unsung attributes.

Salmon tarator

Ingredients

- 4 x 175g skinless, pinboned salmon escalopes
- 1 tablespoon rapeseed oil
- 1 teaspoon lemon salt
- 75g walnuts
- 1 white onion
- 2 tablespoons mint leaves
- 2 teaspoons sumac
- 1 tablespoon pomegranate molasses

Method

- Set the oven to 180°C and lightly oil a baking tray.
- Place the salmon onto the tray, brush half the oil over the top and scatter over the lemon salt.
- Bake for 15 minutes or until firm but with a little 'give'.
- Cool.
- Meanwhile, peel and finely slice the onion, place on a baking tray lined with parchment paper and bush with the remaining tablespoon of oil.
- Roast for 15 minutes.
- Toast the walnuts on a baking tray for 5 minutes.
- When the onions and walnuts are cool, chop them with the mint leaves to a fine crumb.
- Add the sumac and pomegranate molasses.

Paula McIntyre's Down to Earth Cookbook
f i s h

Yoghurt layer

INGREDIENTS

- 75ml local Greek style yoghurt
- 1 tablespoon sesame seeds
- zest 1 lemon
- salt and pepper to taste

METHOD

- Mix all the ingredients together and add salt and pepper.
- Spoon the mixture onto the cooked cool salmon and scatter over the walnut crumb.
- Slice the lemon from the zest into wedges, place around the salmon and scatter with some fresh herbs.

Roast and pickled carrot salad

INGREDIENTS

- 6 medium carrots, scrubbed
- 2 tablespoons rapeseed oil
- few sprigs fresh thyme
- 1 red onion, peeled and finely sliced
- 4 scallions, finely sliced
- 1 clove garlic
- 2 teaspoons honey
- 2 teaspoons Dijon mustard
- 50ml cider vinegar
- juice 1 lemon
- fresh coriander to garnish

METHOD

- Set the oven to 200°C.
- Cut 4 of the carrots in half lengthwise and toss in the oil.
- Season with seasalt and add the thyme sprigs.
- Place on a baking tray and roast, turning occasionally, for about 30 minutes, until soft.
- Peel the remaining carrots, coarsely grate and place in a bowl with the onions and scallions. Season with salt and pepper to taste.
- Crush the garlic with a little salt and place in a bowl.
- Whisk in the honey, mustard, vinegar and lemon juice.
- Toss half into the raw carrot mixture, mix well and place on a platter.
- When the carrots are roasted, toss them into the remaining half of the vinegar mixture.
- Scatter them over the raw carrot mixture and garnish with fresh coriander.

Paula McIntyre's Down to Earth Cookbook

fish

Glenarm salmon tarator with roast and pickled carrot salad

Paula McIntyre's Down to Earth Cookbook
fish

Devilled eggs with smoked salmon

Just like butchers, fishmongers are adding value to fish by curing and smoking it. Northern Irish smoked salmon is a commodity that has been exported around the world. There are fishmongers with generations of experience, alongside a new wave of young artisans, that are producing world class traditional smoked fish and zealously striving to stretch the experimental boundaries.

There seems to be a 1970s feel weaving through this fish section so I'm going to cap it off with the ultimate groovy dish – devilled eggs!

With guilty pleasure I rediscovered them on a recent trip to Kansas and was reminded of their hidden depths and culinary powers of persuasion. They're a slight faff to do but the results are fabulous and a perfect match for the smoked salmon.

Loud shirt and platform heels not obligatory....

Devilled eggs

INGREDIENTS

- 6 good local free range eggs, at room temperature
- 2 tablespoons celery leaves
- 1 teaspoon smoked seasalt
- 1 small red onion, peeled and finely chopped
- 1 tablespoon rapeseed oil
- 1 teaspoon sweet smoked paprika
- 1 gherkin, finely chopped
- 1 teaspoon Dijon mustard
- 35g mayonnaise
- 4 slices chorizo salami

METHOD

- Bring a pan of water to a simmer over medium heat and carefully add the eggs.
- Cook for 10 minutes then run under cold water to cool.
- Place the celery leaves on a baking tray lined with parchment paper and cook at 120°C for 20 minutes or until crisp. Cool, mix into the salt and set aside.
- Cook the onion in the oil until soft and add the paprika. Cook for 20 seconds and cool.
- Peel the eggs and cut in half lengthwise.
- Remove the yolk and place in a bowl.
- Mix in the onion mixture, gherkin, mustard and mayonnaise.
- Spoon or pipe back into the egg white and place on a platter.
- Shred the chorizo and cook in a pan on medium heat until crisp. Drain on kitchen paper and scatter over the eggs.
- Scatter over the celery leaf and salt.
- Serve with hot or cold smoked salmon.

Salted ling brandade with guanciale and smoked local butter

The Slow Food Terra Madre festival takes place in Turin every other year. Around 300 countries are represented at a festival that lasts for 5 days. A stadium the size of 4 football pitches brims with stands, pop up restaurants and lecture halls full of the food, sounds and smells from all the nations exhibiting. The jewel in the crown is the Terra Madre kitchen, a pop up restaurant, with representatives from two selected countries cooking national dishes on a rolling basis, every three hours. I was honoured to represent the UK in 2014, and cooked eels from Lough Neagh with Armagh apples, Peter Hannan from Moira's guanciale (an Italian bacon made from cured pork jowls) and North Coast salt ling brandade, in a kitchen with a group of women chefs from Uganda. David Matchett, originally from Portadown, who now runs the marketing for Borough Market, christened the brandade "fishy champ!" A traditional French dish, it incorporates salt fish, cod in their case, with potatoes and olive oil. My version has salt ling. This is a fish that thrives off the North Coast of Ireland. It is salted to preserve it, then stored up a chimney which imparts an intoxicating smokiness to the mix. This recipe has salt ling and potatoes with the addition of local smoked butter and scallions. It's a delicious bowl of comfort that reinforces the no frills wisdom of our ancestors.

Salt ling

INGREDIENTS

- 500g filleted ling
- 100g seasalt

METHOD

- Rub the salt all over the fish, wrap in cling film and chill for 2 hours.
- Wash off the salt in cold water and pat dry with kitchen paper.

Salt ling brandade

INGREDIENTS

- 500g salt ling as shown above or if you're buying already salted, you'll need to soak in cold water overnight and change the water twice
- 250ml whole milk
- 750g Maris Potatoes, boiled in their jackets, peeled and mashed
- salt to taste
- 4 chopped scallions
- 50g smoked butter

METHOD

- Place the ling in a pan and cover with the milk. Simmer for 10 minutes then add the scallions.
- Cook for a further 5 minutes.
- Flake the fish and mix into the potatoes with the butter.
- Check the seasoning.

6 rashers Peter Hannan's guanciale

METHOD

- Place the guanciale in a dry pan and cook gently until crisp.
- Pat dry and keep the resulting fat for roasties.
- Chop the cooked guanciale and place onto the brandade.
- Great on its own or serve with some pan fried oily fish like salmon or mackerel.

Cider glazed eels with apple and dulse butter, crystallised dulse, and apple and soup celery dressing

When I cook eel, despite initial misgivings, most people are converted. The snakey image doesn't do much for its popularity but once you get over that, the beautiful soft flesh with earthy notes is wonderful. You can buy smoked eels readily now but for fresh silver eel you need to get it from the source at the Fisherman's Cooperative at Toomebridge in County Derry. They'll provide them gutted and you just need to cut them into thumb length pieces. Around the lough shore, eel is still eaten as part of a 'supper' with fried onions and soda farl. My recipe includes apple and dulse, and is one that I cooked at a slow food banquet for 200 people in Bristol in 2015, as part of the Food Connections festival in the city. BBC Radio 4 producer and presenter Dan Saladino hosted the event and is now a champion for this uniquely northern Irish delicacy. The eel and dulse combination even managed to convert a couple of vegetarians.

The sweet apple butter with salty dulse, sweet crisp dulse for texture and the tart apple and savoury soup celery is a perfect combination. Serve with some warm farls.

One tip – cook the eels outside – their oil is quite the pungent thing! Or you could use smoked eel instead – just flash them in a hot pan for 10 seconds and glaze.

Cider glazed eels

INGREDIENTS
- 2 medium sized eels, skinned, gutted and cut into thumb length pieces
- 300ml local cider
- 1 tablespoon honey
- 2 tablespoons cider vinegar

METHOD
- Season the eels with a little salt and place in a frying pan that has been wiped with a teaspoon of rapeseed oil.
- Cook gently, turning them regularly. It will take about 45 minutes to cook them through. I've been told, by people from the shores of Lough Neagh, to treat the eel as if it has eight sides! When you begin to do this, it makes sense, so keep turning them for even cooking.
- In the meantime, place the cider, vinegar and honey in a saucepan and boil until the liquid is syrupy but still runny.
- When the eels have cooked, drain off any fat. Apparently this fat is excellent when rubbed into aching joints – just be careful if you're planning a date night!
- Add the cider mixture and raise the heat.
- Cook to glaze all over.

Apple and dulse butter

INGREDIENTS

- 500g peeled, chopped and cored Armagh cooking apple
- 175g soft brown sugar
- pinch ground clove
- 1 tablespoon dulse, finely chopped

METHOD

- Place the apples in a pan with the sugar and the clove.
- Bring to the boil and simmer gently until the apples are soft.
- Blend and fold in the dulse.

Crystallised dulse

INGREDIENTS

- handful dried dulse
- brown lemonade

METHOD

- Line a baking tray with parchment paper and set the oven to its lowest setting – preferably around 100°C.
- Place about 50ml of brown lemonade in an atomiser. Spray over the dulse. If you don't have an atomiser, just brush the dulse with the lemonade.
- Place in the oven until crisp – about 1 hour.

Apple and soup celery dressing

INGREDIENTS

- 1 teaspoon Dijon mustard
- 1 teaspoon honey
- 25ml cider vinegar
- 75ml local rapeseed oil
- ½ medium Armagh cooking apple
- 2 tablespoons picked soup celery leaves
- salt to taste

METHOD

- Place the mustard in a bowl and whisk in the honey and vinegar.
- Whisk in the oil in a steady stream and then check for seasoning.
- Peel the apple and cut into quarters.
- Core the apple and slice thinly.
- Cut each slice into matchsticks (pile them up to do this as it's quicker) then cut into small dice.
- Add to the dressing and toss around.
- Shred the soup celery leaves as finely as possible and fold into the dressing.
- Place the eel onto a platter, drizzle over the dressing and garnish with the apple butter and dulse.
- Serve with soda farls, buttered liberally.

Paula McIntyre's Down to Earth Cookbook

fish

Cider glazed eels with apple and dulse butter, crystallised dulse, and apple and soup celery dressing

Paula McIntyre's Down to Earth Cookbook
fish

Dollaghan or brown trout almondine

Dollaghan or brown trout almondine

As a young child I was obsessed with restaurants – the smells, sounds and big chef hats! My parents used to get complimented on how well my brother and I behaved. The fact was we both loved eating out so much that we were terrified it wouldn't happen again if we weren't as good as gold! Nothing much has changed – I still get a buzz from trying out a new restaurant. We're beginning to embrace the fish eating thing here now but back in the 1970s the token gesture on menus was often limited to cod mornay and trout with almonds. And this in a time of no overfishing and abundant stocks! These classic dishes are both out of favour now and while I agree that clarrying a nice piece of cod with stodgy cheese sauce should be outlawed as a crime against cooking, trout with almonds shouldn't. This was one of the first things I cooked in Harry Magee's class in the College of Business studies in Belfast. Harry was a dapper man who wore a white coat, dicky bow and matching handkerchief. He could fillet a trout, cook it and never have a hair out of place. I still try to emulate his perfectionism! And trout cooked in butter with crunchy almonds and a hint of citrus truly is perfect!

INGREDIENTS

- 2 trout fillets, skinned and pin boned
- 1 tablespoon local rapeseed oil
- 1 shallot, peeled and finely chopped
- 50g butter
- zest and juice 1 lemon
- handful chopped parsley
- 1 tablespoon elderberry capers (recipe on page 125), substitute with regular capers, chopped, or omit
- 25g toasted flaked almonds

METHOD

- Heat the oil in a non stick pan until very hot. Season the fillets with salt and place in the pan.
- Seal off for 30 seconds, lower the heat and add half the butter and the shallot.
- Cook until the shallots are golden (about 2 minutes) then flip the fish over.
- Add the lemon juice and zest, elderberry capers and parsley.
- Add the remaining butter and check the seasoning.
- Cook through and then transfer to plates to serve.
- Spoon over all the juices and top with the toasted almonds.
- It's lovely with some new potatoes.

Smoked salmon fishcakes with horseradish and smoked black pepper dressing

There are excellent fish smokehouses dotted around Northern Ireland. When they smoke a side of salmon, they trim it down and invariably sell the trimmings at a vastly cheaper price. When you make them into a fish cake with soft, fluffy potatoes encased in crispy breadcrumbs, they are luxuriously exquisite. Ruaridh Morrison is an Islay native, now based in Ballycastle, who hot smokes salmon, salt and black pepper. Paring his smoked black pepper with hot horseradish in a creamy sauce, makes for a deliciously peppy sauce for the smoky fishcakes.

Smoked salmon fishcakes

INGREDIENTS

- 450g potatoes
- 300g smoked salmon trimmings
- 2 scallions, chopped finely
- handful of chopped parsley
- salt and pepper
- 2 eggs
- 50g plain flour
- 100g breadcrumbs
- oil for frying

METHOD

- Boil the potatoes until soft, drain, return to the pan and dry out well.
- Mash and place in a bowl.
- Add the salmon, scallions and parsley, and season to taste.
- Form into 8 shapes using a scone cutter and place in the fridge to chill for 1 hour.
- Dip each one in flour, shake off the excess and dip in the egg, coating completely.
- Dredge in the crumbs to completely cover.
- Heat half a thumbnail depth of oil in a frying pan over medium heat.
- When a little bit of bread fizzles when added to the pan, add the fishcakes and cook for about 5 minutes on each side.
- Serve with fresh leaves, fresh lemon wedges and the horseradish and smoked black pepper dressing.

Horseradish and smoked black pepper dressing

INGREDIENTS

- 125g crème fraîche
- 2 tablespoons mayonnaise
- zest and juice 1 lemon
- 1 tablespoon horseradish sauce
- 2 teaspoons North Coast Smokehouse smoked black pepper

METHOD

- Whisk together all the ingredients and season with a little salt if you wish.

Lough Neagh pollan with mealie crushie

In their first incarnation pollan were herring, trapped in Lough Neagh during the last ice age. They're a fresh water fish, but look like sea herring. When you fillet them you don't get the ozoney smell you do from sea fish, but instead a fresh, mossy, earthy aroma. When I see them on a menu my heart skips, but it's a rare thing. Speak to anyone who's tried pollan and they get nostalgic and a bit choked up! I remember shopping in Cookstown with my Granny Kathleen, where, on market day, she would buy pollan from the fisherman selling them from buckets on the street. She was a health visitor in Coalisland so invariably knew the sellers well, and always got a bit extra free! She fried the fish and we guzzled them with bread and butter. To this day it's one of the simplest and most evocative food memories I have.

Mealie crushie is an old dish of oats fried in bacon fat. Herring, oats and bacon is perfect together – for the deluxe version add pollan.

INGREDIENTS

- 4 rashers of dry cure streaky bacon
- 2 tablespoons local rapeseed oil
- 8 medium pollan fillets
- ½ teaspoon seasalt
- 25g butter
- 50g porridge oats
- 2 finely chopped scallions
- 2 tablespoons finely chopped parsley

METHOD

- Heat the oven to 200°C.
- Cook the bacon in one tablespoon of the oil, in a pan over a gentle heat until crisp and golden.
- Remove the bacon from pan and pat dry on kitchen paper.
- Place the pollan on a lightly oiled baking tray, skin side up.
- Drizzle over the remaining oil and season with the salt.
- Place in the oven for 5 minutes.
- Add the butter to the bacon pan. When melted add the oats and scallions and cook over a medium heat until toasted.
- Add the parsley, chop the cooked bacon and add to the mix.
- Plate up the fish and scatter over the mealie crushie.
- Serve with warm buttered soda farls.

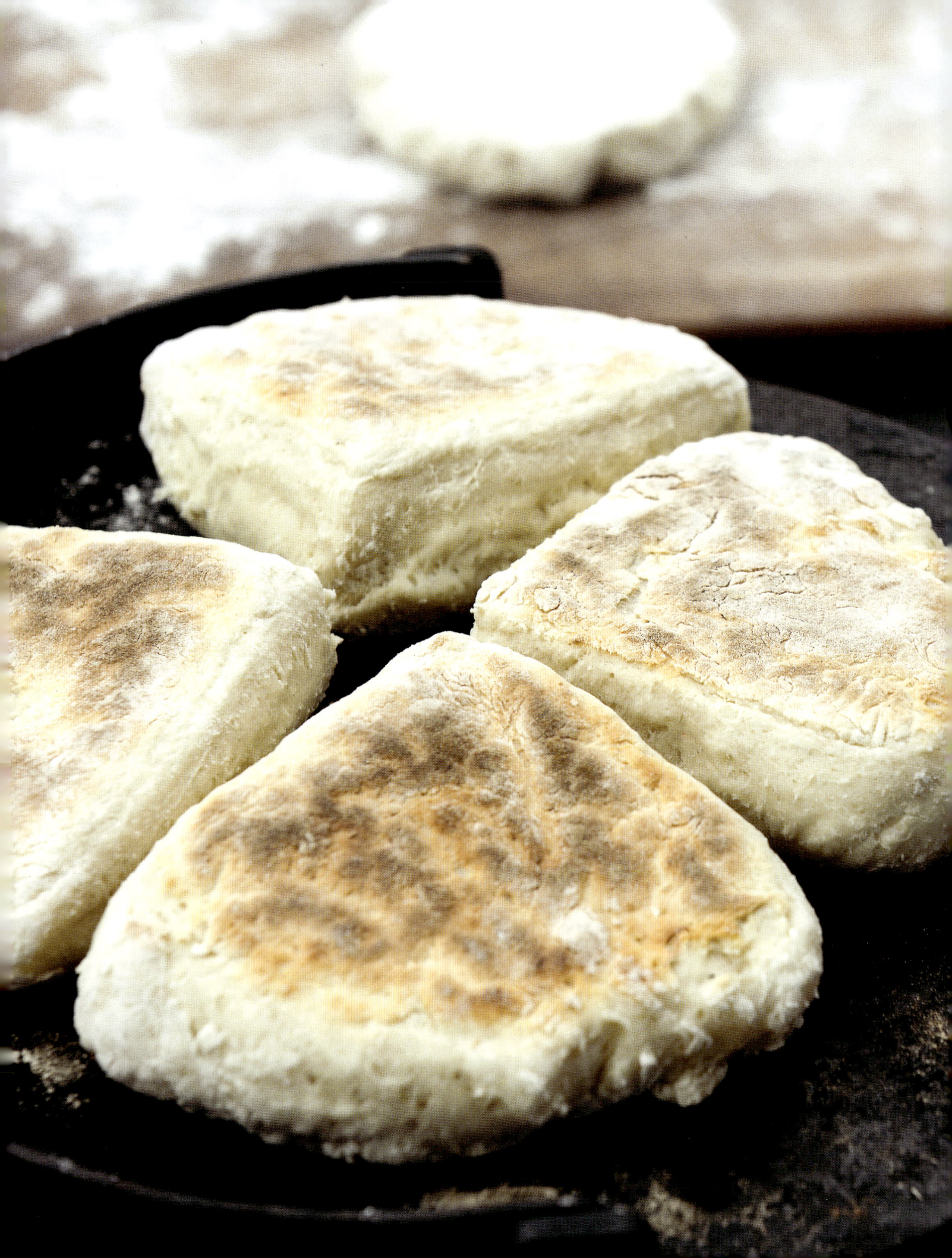

CHAPTER FIVE

Bread

In Northern Ireland we are fortuitous in having a unique and indigenous style of bread known as the soda farl. The word farl means a quarter and comes from the same derivative as the farthing coin. Flour with the addition of baking soda and salt is mixed to a soft dough with buttermilk. After being gently coaxed together, flattened and cut into 4 quarters, it's placed on a hot griddle and gently cooked. The smell of buttermilk and scorched flour is one that's etched on the mind of many an over 40 year old in this country. When you visit the Rectory at the Ulster Folk and Transport Museum in Cultra, outside Belfast, they will make soda farls on a griddle over a turf fire, just like our ancestors did hundreds of years ago. Slightly smoky, warm bread, slathered with butter alone is worth the trip to Northern Ireland!

Having been raised in a rural community, baking bread was a daily ritual in our house and many others. My mother and granny both baked wheaten bread and as a special treat we had pancakes at the weekend, fresh off the griddle. It's unfortunate that this once common practice has all but died out. When you use basic, good ingredients like flour and buttermilk, you know exactly where you stand. A wheaten bread is amazing when served straight from the oven with butter but deteriorates within a couple of days if you don't eat it. It frightens me to see the unnaturally long sell by dates on packaged bread – they must be saturated in e-numbers and sugar to stay 'fresh' for that long.

The first thing I ever baked was a tealoaf at my granny's house outside Cookstown. I was 4 years old and needed a stool to reach the bench. It wasn't yesterday but I remember it like it was. I've found that children like to get down and dirty with any kind of cooking, and seem much more inclined to eat bread if they've had a hand in baking it. Pancakes are great introduction for young people and gives them a basic understanding of the process involved.

I had my paternal granny's griddle for years but warped it making soft flour tortillas on too high a heat! One morning I mentioned this on BBC Radio Ulster and a listener from Newmills, Margaret Gamble, phoned the programme to say I could have hers. It's been with me ever since and lives permanently in the boot of my car! The thick, heavy set iron makes the heat distribution ideal for griddle breads and I love that I use a piece of history to continue the Ulster bread making tradition.

With the exception of two, the recipes in this chapter use the flour, baking soda and buttermilk technique, with a few added extras. These are breads that can be whipped up and baked within an hour, no need for resting or extreme kneading. The recipes for walnut bread and pretzel rolls are included because they're delicious – a bit more work involved but completely worth it.

When you make bread with your own hands and serve it straight from the oven to your loved ones it's like presenting them with a beautiful gift and a recollection to cherish.

Pancakes

When I was growing up, our next door neighbour, Mrs Hunter was a prolific baker. She made sodas, slims (a thinner soda with the addition of dried fruit) and pancakes every day. Her grandson, James, and I used to stand beside the cooker while she doled out the pancakes, which we spread with butter and sprinkled with sugar. I'm sure we ate 12 each at a sitting and she never once complained. I tried to get the recipe from her but she worked in handfuls rather than specific measurements. This recipe is as near to the original as I can get and the one I make for any young visitors!

Ingredients

- 3 large eggs
- 1 dessertspoon golden syrup
- 200ml buttermilk
- 300g self raising soda bread flour
- 1 tablespoon castor sugar
- oil for cooking

Method

- Whisk the eggs and syrup in a bowl and mix in the buttermilk.
- Sift in the flour and add the castor sugar. Whisk to a thick batter.
- Allow to rest for 10 minutes. At this stage you could add raisins, dried fruit, chopped apples or spices.
- When ready to cook, wipe a medium hot pan with some oil on a piece of kitchen paper.
- Drop tablespoons of the batter onto the pan, allowing a bit of space between them. When bubbles appear on the surface, flip over and cook for another minute on the other side.
- Repeat with the remaining batter and cool the cooked ones on a wire rack.
- Butter and drizzle with honey to serve.

Paula McIntyre's Down to Earth Cookbook
bread

Pancakes

Paula McIntyre's Down to Earth Cookbook
bread

Walnut bread with salted grapes and rosemary

Walnut bread with salted grapes and rosemary

'Blessed are cheesemakers' should be the ninth beatitude. We have an abundance of skilled cheesemakers right across the province. With access to the best milk in the world, they produce limited batches of artisan products that have a won an abundance of awards at global cheese competitions.

The combination of nuts, grapes and cheese is a trusted one and this bread combines these natural companions. Warm, nutty bread, dotted with sweet and salty grapes is delicious with any cheese.

Ingredients

- 500g strong bread flour
- 75g finely chopped walnuts
- 2 sachets instant yeast
- 1 teaspoon salt
- 1 tablespoon honey
- 50ml rapeseed oil
- 175ml local dry cider
- 200ml lukewarm water
- 250g red grapes
- 1 tablespoon fresh rosemary leaves
- 1 teaspoon seasalt

Method

- Mix the flour, walnuts, yeast and salt in a bowl.
- Whisk the honey, oil, cider and water.
- Mix into the dry ingredients to a loose dough.
- Turn onto a floured surface and knead for 5–10 minutes or until it starts to become elastic and takes more effort to knead. You could do this in your food mixer with the dough hook attachment.
- Cover with a damp teatowel and leave to double in size – this takes about 1 hour.
- Knock back the dough – literally stick your fist into the middle!
- Lightly flour a baking tin.
- Place the dough on a floured surface, roll into a ball then flatten to a round about 2cm thick and place in the baking tin.
- Cut the grapes in half and place cut side up into the dough.
- Scatter over the rosemary and seasalt and allow to rest for half an hour.
- During this time preset the oven to 200°C.
- Bake the bread for about 30 minutes.
- Cool for 10 minutes then serve with cheese and chutney.

Rousel bread

Rousel bread is a traditional bread from the East Antrim region. Essentially it's a potato bread, also known as fadge, with the addition of oats. Potato bread is part of our culture and integral to the world famous Ulster fry. I've cooked this many times and people respond fondly to it but I've never managed to get the spelling confirmed, so please excuse the artistic licence – it doesn't affect the taste!

Ingredients

- 250g mashed potatoes (roughly two large potatoes)
- 15g butter
- 50g plain flour
- 50g oats
- pinch of sugar
- ½ teaspoon salt

Method

- Mix the butter into the hot potatoes, followed by the flour, oats, sugar and salt.
- Turn onto a floured surface and knead together.
- Roll out to just less than 1cm thick.
- Cut into squares or triangles and place on a hot griddle or frying pan.
- Cook for about 2 minutes each side.
- Cool on a wire rack.

To finish...

- At this stage you can eat them warm with butter but they taste even better fried with bacon.
- Fry off some good quality bacon and fry the rousel in the remaining fat until golden and crisp.

Wheaten bread

In the 1990s I owned a restaurant in Manchester and baked wheaten bread, to my Granny's recipe, every day. Panic initially set in when I discovered English buttermilk is nothing like you get here and was too thick and yoghurt like for the recipe. A phonecall to Granny concluded that milk with vinegar added would do the job, and worked a treat. I always left it late in the day to bake the bread so it would be warm from the oven and still have the lingering smell permeating through the restaurant when the customers arrived. I've tweaked the recipe a bit but the elements of wholemeal flour, butter, treacle and brown sugar remain the same. Now I bake it like a cob and add some oats to the mix but the essence is still there. Sliced while warm and spread with butter, in my mind this must be like what the honey bees experience when they collect nectar.

INGREDIENTS

- 50g butter
- 50g treacle
- 250g wholemeal flour
- 1 teaspoon salt
- 15g Demerara sugar
- 75g oats
- 125g self raising flour
- 1 and half teaspoons baking soda
- 275ml buttermilk

METHOD

- Set the oven to 210°C.
- Melt the butter and treacle in a pan together and cool.
- Mix the wholemeal flour, salt, sugar, oats and self raising flour in a bowl. Sift in the baking soda and mix well.
- Make a well in the centre and add the buttermilk and treacle mixture.
- Mix to a soft dough and place on a floured surface.
- Roll into a ball and place on a floured baking tray.
- Flatten the dough slightly and slash a cross into the middle.
- Bake for 15 minutes at 210°C then lower the heat to 160°C and continue to cook for about another 25 minutes or until the bottom sounds hollow when tapped.
- Cool slightly on a wire rack.

Treacle soda farls

Sticky, tar like treacle adds rich, sweet and bitter notes to baking. Ginger cake would not have the same appeal without the addition of treacle and by the same token it adds so much to a traditional soda farl. Farls, are deep rooted in our bread culture in Northern Ireland. You won't find this indigenous staple anywhere else except here. The recipe is simple, taking plain flour, salt and baking soda, and mixing with buttermilk to a soft dough.

It is then gently coaxed into a flat round, cut into quarters and cooked gently on a griddle. Adding some treacle gives the bread a splendid amber glow and a tangy, honey like taste.

INGREDIENTS

- 350g self raising soda bread flour
- pinch salt
- 1 tablespoon treacle
- 325ml buttermilk

METHOD

- Mix the flour and salt in a bowl and make a well in the centre.
- Whisk the treacle and buttermilk together and pour into the well.
- Mix to a soft dough and place on a floured surface. Knead gently into a ball and flatten to 2cm thick.
- Cut into 4 or cut in half and then cut each half in 4 for a more compact soda.
- Leave for 5 minutes while you heat up your griddle or a couple of frying pans (it's important the farls have room to spread slightly) to medium heat.
- Add the farls and leave for 4 minutes. Flip over and cook for roughly the same on the other side – when they sound hollow when you tap them, they're ready.
- Cool slightly on a wire rack, split open and spread with butter and jam.
- They're also really good with some smoked or fresh poached salmon.

Paula McIntyre's Down to Earth Cookbook
bread

Treacle soda farls

Paula McIntyre's Down to Earth Cookbook
bread

Yoghurt flatbread with gorse flowers and black pepper

Yoghurt flatbread with gorse flowers and black pepper

This recipe is one inspired by my friend, and amazing baker, the late David Semple. He fermented a sour dough starter and then used it to make flatbreads. My version uses yoghurt, which is simpler, and warm water. The mixture is left at room temperature for a couple of hours to work its magic then rolled into misshapen pieces and cooked for a couple of minutes on a hot pan or barbecue. David added gorse flowers for colour and flavour. The addition of black pepper here gives the floral delicacy a little kick.

Ingredients

- 350g self raising flour
- 2 tablespoons local Greek style yoghurt
- 1 tablespoon rapeseed oil
- 1 tablespoon chopped gorse flowers
- 1 teaspoon freshly cracked black pepper
- ½ teaspoon salt
- 200ml lukewarm water

Method

- Place the flour in a bowl and make a well in the centre.
- Add the yoghurt, oil, gorse, pepper and salt, along with the water.
- Mix to a soft dough and cover with cling film.
- Set aside in a warm place for an hour.
- Place the dough on a floured surface and knead together.
- Divide into 6 pieces and roll each piece into a ball.
- Using either a rolling pin or your fingers form the balls into oval shapes, about ½cm thick.
- Place on a hot frying pan. When bubbles appear on the surface of the dough, flip over and cook for another minute on the other side.
- It's great served hot with natural yoghurt mixed with chopped fresh mint.

Soda bread with onions, cheese and scallions

This crusty white bread, with a soft pillowy middle, is made in a similar way to wheaten bread – buttermilk and baking soda to create the rise, a good hot scorch for the initial 10 minutes of cooking then lowered to cook through slowly.

It's a quick bread to prepare and the results are stunning. Eat when still warm with butter and after a couple of days toasted to give another dimension. A handful of fruit and a shake of spice can be added to the mix as well. In this case I've gone down the savoury route with onions and cheese in the mix.

INGREDIENTS

- 450g self raising soda bread flour
- 1 teaspoon salt
- 2 onions, peeled and finely sliced
- 1 tablespoon rapeseed oil
- 4 chopped scallions
- 50g sharp mature cheddar, grated
- 450ml buttermilk

METHOD

- Set the oven to 220°C.
- Place the flour and salt in a bowl.
- Fry the onions in the oil until soft and golden.
- Allow to cool.
- Make a well in the centre and add the cooked onions, scallions and cheese.
- Pour in the buttermilk and mix to a smooth dough.
- Turn onto a floured surface and form into a ball.
- Place on a floured baking tray, flatten slightly and slash a cross in the middle of the dough.
- Bake for 10 minutes at 220°C.
- Lower the heat to 160°C and continue to cook for about 25 minutes or until the bottom of the bread sounds hollow when tapped.
- Cool on a wire rack.
- Serve hot or toast if keeping for a few days.

Pretzel rolls

Early in 2015 I was delighted to be asked to be a judge on the BBC Radio 4 Food and Farming Awards, in the street food category. The ultimate winners were Hangfire Smokehouse in Wales. One of the partners in the business, Shauna Gunn, is originally from Belfast, and I was blown away by their delicious barbecued ribs, brisket, sauces and accompaniments. Their pulled pork, with pickled jalapenos and pretzel rolls was the taste equivalent of front row seats at a James Taylor concert! This is my version of the rolls – the effort involved includes poaching the uncooked rolls in a baking soda solution first but the result is magnificent and unforgettable.

INGREDIENTS

- 100g butter
- 2½ teaspoons dried active yeast
- 10g castor sugar
- 325ml lukewarm water
- ½ teaspoon salt
- 525g strong bread flour
- 50g baking soda
- 1 egg yolk
- 2 teaspoons coarse seasalt

METHOD

- Melt the butter and allow to cool.
- Place the yeast, sugar and water in a bowl and leave for 10 minutes until it froths up.
- Add the butter, flour and salt, and mix to a dough. You could do this in a food mixer with the dough hook attachment – allow to run on medium speed for 5 minutes. Alternatively, turn onto a lightly floured board and knead for 10 minutes.
- Cover with a damp teatowel or cling film and leave for an hour.
- Knock back the dough – literally stick your fist into the middle!
- Place on a floured board and cut into 12 pieces – if you want to be really precise, weigh them.
- Roll each into a ball and place on a baking tray lined with parchment paper.
- Cover with a teatowel and leave for 30 minutes.
- Set the oven to 200°C.
- Bring 2 litres of water to the boil in a saucepan. Carefully add the baking soda – stir to stop it fizzing all over the place.
- With the pan on a simmer, place the rolls, seam side down, in batches of 3 into the water. After 30 seconds, turn over and poach for another 30 seconds.
- Remove with a slotted spoon onto a tray.
- Place on a tray dusted with polenta or flour and slash twice on top.
- Brush with the egg yolk and sprinkle over the salt.
- Bake for about 20 minutes, turning around once to get an even cooking, or until they sound hollow when you tap the bottom.
- Cool on a wire rack.

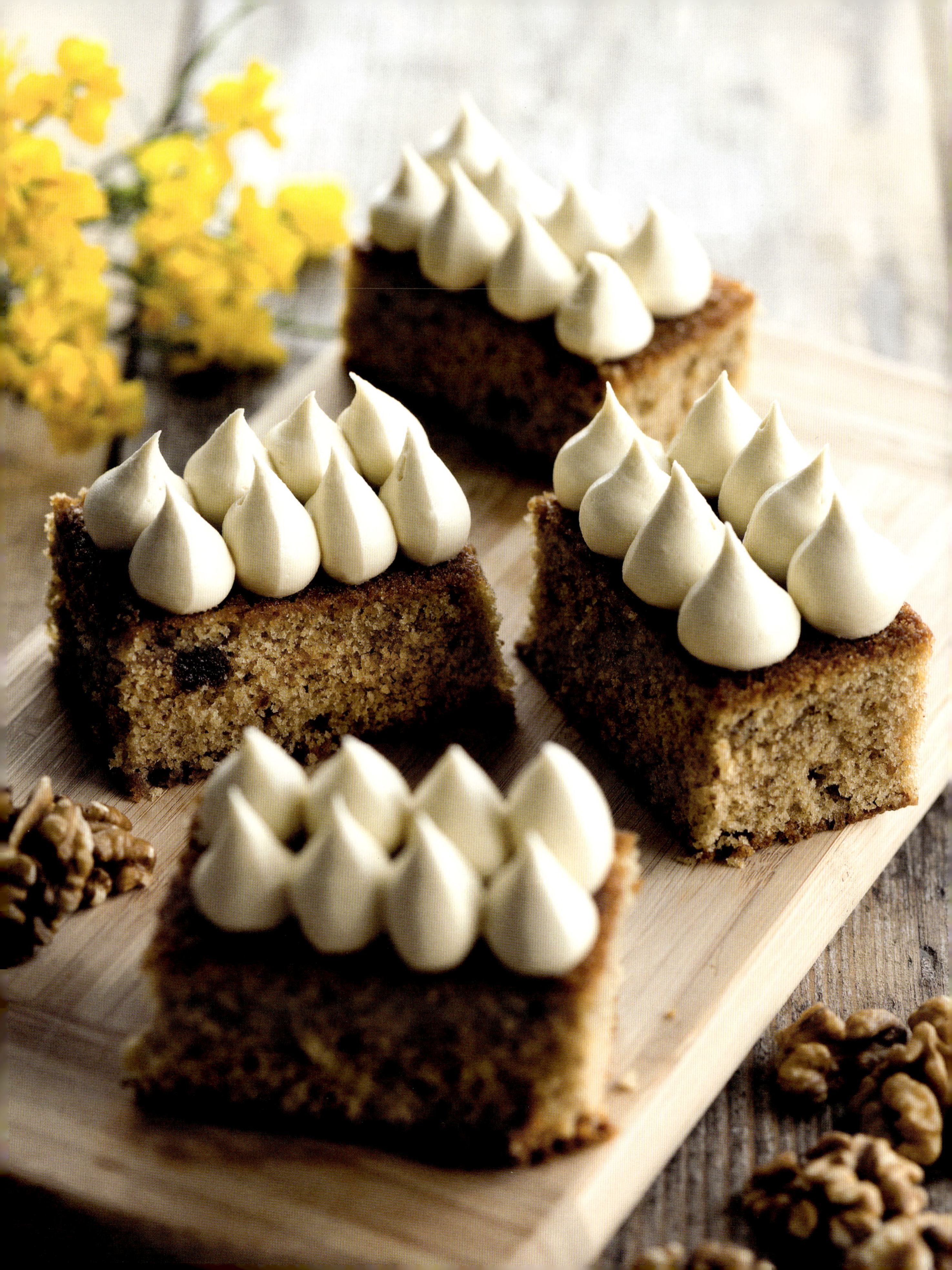

CHAPTER SIX

Sweets and Treats

The need for something sweet is one thing that binds us together in this country. No birth, baptism, engagement, wedding or funeral would be quite the same without a traybake or sticky confection to accompany the obligatory tea. At times of happiness, sadness or crisis, the kettle will be put on and the buns produced. Fifteens are the first 'cooking' experience for most children here. Small, sticky fingers religiously count out the requisite number of mallows, digestives and cherries to chop, fold in condensed milk and roll in coconut to misshapen sausage like treats.

The Women's Institute is synonymous with good baking and their cookbooks, which have spanned decades, have been the ultimate recipe guide for reliable cakes, traybakes and breads. The recipes work beautifully because they've been tried and tested and no self respecting member would put their name to something that wouldn't turn out right. I don't often get nervous doing cookery demonstrations but always have a flutter in my stomach before I face a group of WI members – my rustic style sometimes is not in tandem with their exacting standards! I don't sweat over the dimensions when cutting my traybakes.

When I lived in Manchester, my mum and a friend came over to stay and we bought some buns and biscuits to have with tea. You can take the girls out of Northern Ireland but can't take the Northern Ireland out of the girls! We couldn't have been more disappointed – the shortcake and iced buns were awful and nothing like those we cooked or bought in the bakeries at home. Bakeries here have bucked the economic trend and are flourishing, with their standards only improving over the years.

At times of austerity we can give up a lot of things but a sweet treat now and again is never going to be one of them. Fermanagh, Tyrone, Armagh, Derry, Down and Antrim are all blessed with exceeding good home bakeries! The smell of freshly baked loaves, scorched flour, resulting in apple turnovers, donkey's lugs, doughnuts and French fancies transports you back to a simpler, easier time. When you buy a half soda or wheaten cob in a good bakery, it won't be full of additives and will have been made with generations of skill, love and precision. We should cherish these talented bakers.

My aunt, Doreen Cochrane, who was a home economics teacher in Coleraine, is my go to traybake and baking guru. Everything she makes is as light as a feather and packed with flavour. I've included a couple of her recipes and some of my own that I've gathered over the years that are fail safe and reliable.

Baking is something that has brought generations together in the past, it transcends age and social mores and needs to be nurtured and shared as much as possible.

Paula McIntyre's Down to Earth Cookbook

sweets and treats

My Aunt Doreen's Chinese chews

During my childhood we would regularly visit my dad's sister Doreen and my late Uncle Johnny in Portstewart on Sunday afternoons. My parents, Doreen and Johnny were all teachers and they would discuss the defects of the education system while us children would look on, roll our eyes and eat most of Doreen's traybake supply for the month. I live in Portstewart now and it's my turn to visit Doreen and complain about the demise of the education system!

She still has a great selection of traybakes but this is a firm favourite – a crispy biscuity base with a spice, fruit and date spongey topping.

INGREDIENTS

- 100g soft butter
- 100g light brown sugar
- 2 eggs
- 50g self raising flour
- 150g chopped dates
- 1 teaspoon chopped preserved ginger
- ½ teaspoon ground cinnamon
- 75g chopped mixed nuts

METHOD

- Set the oven to 180°C.
- Grease a swiss roll tin and line with parchment paper.
- Cream the butter and sugar until pale and fluffy.
- Add the eggs one at a time.
- Mix in the flour, followed by the remaining ingredients.
- Spread into the lined tin.
- Bake for 30 minutes or until spongey on top and golden brown.
- Remove from the oven, sprinkle with castor sugar and cut into squares.

Paula McIntyre's Down to Earth Cookbook
sweets and treats

My Aunt Doreen's Chinese chews

Doreen's oat biscuits with whiskey soaked raisins

Flakemeal biscuits are a traditional treat in Ulster. They're crisp and melt in your mouth. I decided to experiment with the family recipe and add some whiskey soaked raisins. This transforms them into a cookie shaped biscuit rather than the uniform flakemeal style. You can leave out the raisins and have a traditional variation (Doreen sometimes substitutes 25g of coconut for the oats) or go a bit wild and add the raisins – 2 recipes for the price of 1!

INGREDIENTS

- 25g raisins
- 50ml whiskey
- 100g soft butter
- 50g castor sugar
- 50g plain flour
- 125g porridge oats
- pinch baking soda
- 1 teaspoon vanilla extract

METHOD

- Soak the raisins in the whiskey overnight.
- Set the oven to 170°C.
- Beat the butter and sugar until pale and fluffy.
- Fold in the flour, porridge oats and baking soda.
- Mix in the soaked raisins and vanilla.
- Line 2 baking trays with parchment paper.
- Roll out the dough on a lightly floured surface to about ½cm, ¼ inch thick.
- Cut out into shapes with a pastry cutter and place on the trays. Make sure they're not too close as they'll spread.
- Bake for 15–20 minutes or until golden.
- Cool on the tray for 5 minutes before transferring to a cooling rack.
- Serve when cool or keep in an airtight container.

Gluten free carrot cake with cinnamon icing

Richard Kane is a cereal and potato farmer based on the Broighter Road outside Limavady. His wife Leona was frying steaks one night and ran out of olive oil. Richard had just pressed some of the rapeseed he grows into a biofuel and suggested she use it for cooking. They loved the nutty, fresh taste of the oil and Leona proposed that they bottle and sell it for culinary use instead. Appropriately they named it after a hoard of Viking gold that had been found on the farm in 1896. In the last 5 years they've won numerous awards for their Broighter Gold rapeseed oils. There's nothing like a good carrot cake and this gluten free version uses Leona's lemon flavoured oil in the recipe to great effect.

Carrot cake

INGREDIENTS

- 150g soft brown sugar
- 150ml Broighter Gold lemon rapeseed oil or vegetable oil
- 3 eggs
- 150g gluten free self raising flour
- ½ teaspoon baking soda
- 125g coarsely grated carrots
- 1 teaspoon ground cinnamon
- 35g chopped dried pineapple
- 50g raisins
- 25g desiccated coconut

METHOD

- Set the oven to 180°C.
- Lightly oil and line a baking tin with parchment paper.
- Whisk the sugar, oil and eggs together.
- Sift the flour and baking soda together.
- Mix the dry mixture into the wet, along with the carrots.
- Mix in the cinnamon, pineapple, raisins and coconut.
- Pour into the tin and bake for 45 minutes or until an inserted skewer comes out clean.
- Cool in the tin for 15 minutes then transfer to a cooling rack.
- Cool completely before icing.

Cinnamon icing

INGREDIENTS

- 250g full fat cream cheese
- 50g icing sugar
- 2 teaspoons ground cinnamon
- 1 teaspoon vanilla extract

METHOD

- Whisk together and spread or pipe over the carrot cake.

Paula McIntyre's Down to Earth Cookbook
sweets and treats

Chocolate truffles

Chocolate truffles

This is a recipe that just keeps on giving. You can add whatever flavourings your heart desires and it makes loads of bite sized balls – perfect as an after dinner treat or to bring as a gift. Buy good quality dark chocolate. My favourite way of doing these is using local whiskey and then rolling the finished truffles in crushed honeycomb (recipe on page 118) but adapt them to your taste and reap the rewards.

INGREDIENTS

- 1 tablespoon liquid glucose
- 1 tablespoon honey
- 100ml double cream
- 25ml liqueur
- 250g good quality, dark chocolate, chopped
- 75g soft butter, chopped

METHOD

- Place the glucose, honey, cream and liqueur in a saucepan and bring to a gentle simmer.
- Place the chocolate and butter in a heat proof bowl, and add the hot cream mixture.
- Stir until the chocolate is melted.
- At this stage either pour the mixture into a cling film lined tray (so you can cut out cubes) or just chill the bowl so you can make balls later.
- Dip a melon baller into boiling water and scoop out balls.
- Roll in cocoa, toasted coconut or crushed honeycomb.
- Serve with coffee or after dinner liqueur.

Paula McIntyre's Down to Earth Cookbook

sweets and treats

Rocky road

This is a souped up, adult version of this popular traybake. It involves making marshmallow, which I love because it's a fantastic way of using up excess egg whites. Frozen cherries are readily available but you could substitute with fresh raspberries. You can freeze this very successfully and it's perfect served with coffee or tea instead of dessert.

Marshmallow

INGREDIENTS

- 200g stoned fresh cherries or frozen cherries, soaked in 150ml rum
- 5 leaves gelatine
- 2 tablespoons icing sugar
- 1 tablespoon cornflour
- 225g castor sugar
- 1 tablespoon liquid glucose
- 1 large egg white (at room temperature)

METHOD

- When the cherries are well soaked, drain the juice and make sure you have 225ml.
- Soak the gelatine in cold water.
- Line a baking tray with parchment paper.
- Mix the icing sugar and cornflour together and dust half over the bottom of the tray.
- Put the liquid glucose, reserved cherry liquor and sugar into a pan and bring to the boil.
- Boil until the mixture reaches 127°C on a thermometer or until a small drop, placed in cold water, forms a soft pliable ball.
- Whisk the egg white until stiff and while still beating, slowly pour in the hot liquid in a steady stream.
- When all the liquid is added, squeeze the water from the gelatine and add to the hot egg white mixture.
- Continue to whisk until the mixture is cool.
- Spoon the mixture into the tray and smooth over the top.
- Dust with the remaining icing sugar and cornflour mixture and chill to set.
- When the marshmallow is set chop half of it – you can freeze the rest.

Rocky road

INGREDIENTS

- 200g good quality, dark chocolate, chopped
- 125g butter
- 2 tablespoons honey
- 200g shortcake biscuits
- 50g coarsely chopped pistachio nuts

METHOD

- Line a baking tray with parchment paper.
- Chop the reserved cherries.
- Melt the butter and chocolate in a heat proof bowl, over a pan of gently simmering water. Ensure the bottom of the bowl and the water don't touch, as it will cause the chocolate to seize.
- Crush the biscuits coarsely – put them in a plastic bag and beat them with a rolling pin.
- Fold them into the chocolate mixture with the pistachios, chopped marshmallow and reserved cherries.
- Press into the baking tin and chill to set.
- Cut into bite sized pieces to serve.

Paula McIntyre's Down to Earth Cookbook
sweets and treats

Paula McIntyre's Down to Earth Cookbook
sweets and treats

Buttermilk cake

A few summers ago I visited a community group in Carnlough and had the pleasure of watching them make butter. It reminded me of the Seamus Heaney poem *Churning Day* and inspired this golden crusted buttermilk cake.

At the festival in Seamus's honour, in Magherafelt, in 2014, I developed this cake to use both handchurned butter and the residual buttermilk. The smell of buttermilk and vanilla together in the batter is as good as the finished cake!

It's nice on its own with a cup of tea but to elevate it for this illustrious occasion I added elderflower poached rhubarb, cream and a sprinkling of honeycomb.

INGREDIENTS

- 190g soft butter
- 330g castor sugar
- 3 large eggs
- 210g plain flour
- 1 teaspoon baking powder
- 125ml buttermilk
- 1 teaspoon vanilla extract

METHOD

- Set the oven to 180°C.
- Grease and line an 25cm, 10 inch, cake tin with parchment paper.
- Beat the butter and sugar until pale and fluffy. This will take about 10 minutes with an electric beater.
- Add the eggs one at a time, while still whisking.
- Mix the flour and baking powder, and fold half into the butter mixture along with half the buttermilk. When incorporated, fold in the remaining flour mixture, buttermilk and vanilla.
- Spoon into the cake tin and smooth off the top.
- Bake for about 45 minutes or until golden and firm on top and an inserted skewer comes out clean.
- Cool in the tin for 10 minutes, turn out and serve warm or cold.
- Store in an airtight container for up to 3 days.

Elderflower poached rhubarb

Seamus Heaney, the Nobel Laureate poet from Bellaghy in County Derry, mentions the elder bush in his poems regularly. He uses the old name, the 'boortree bush'. Summer rhubarb and elderflowers have a natural affinity. You can use shop bought cordial or make your own in season (recipe on page 126) The addition of grenadine brings out the natural colour in the rhubarb and adds just the right amount of sweetness.

INGREDIENTS

- 4 sticks rhubarb, preferably red
- 150g castor sugar
- 50ml elderflower cordial
- 100ml water or dry cider
- 2 tablespoons grenadine

METHOD

- Set the oven to 160°C.
- Cut the rhubarb into 3cm sized sticks.
- Place in a baking dish large enough that they're not piled up to ensure even cooking.
- Boil the sugar, cordial, water and grenadine until the sugar has dissolved.
- Pour over the rhubarb, cover with parchment paper and bake until just cooked but intact.
- Cool.
- Strain off most of the liquid – it's brilliant added to chilled sparkling wine, dry cider or lemonade for a fruity cocktail.

Homemade mincemeat pies

This recipe came about because of my complete and life long aversion to candied peel. The only way to avoid it in mincemeat is to make your own. Invariably this is infinitely better than anything out of a jar.

It calls for butter instead of suet which also makes it vegetarian.

For health and safety reasons, I'm going to say store it in a jar in the fridge for up to a month but the reality is that I sometimes make an apple and mincemeat tart in mid summer when I find a rogue jar at the back of the fridge!

Mincemeat

INGREDIENTS

- 100g ice cold butter, coarsely grated
- 200g dark brown sugar
- 2 Armagh Bramley apples, peeled, cored and coarsely grated
- zest and juice 1 lemon
- zest and juice 1 orange
- 50ml Grand Marnier or orange liqueur
- 150ml Port
- 100ml Brandy
- 600g dried mixed fruit – I like a mixture of dried cranberries, cherries, figs, sultanas, pear and raisins
- 2 teaspoons mixed spice
- 1 round preserved ginger, finely chopped
- 2 teaspoons ground cinnamon
- 1 teaspoon ground cloves

METHOD

- Place everything in a bowl and mix well with your hands to incorporate all the ingredients.
- Place in sterilised jam jars, seal with a lid and leave for at least 3 days before using.

Clementine pastry

INGREDIENTS

- 225g plain flour
- 150g cold butter, diced
- 75g castor sugar
- 2 egg yolks
- zest 1 clementine
- 1 tablespoon ice cold water

METHOD

- Rub the flour and butter together, with or without a food processor, until the mixture resembles fine crumbs.
- Add the sugar and mix well.
- Mix one of the egg yolks with the zest and water, and add this to the crumbs to form a dough.
- Wrap in cling film and chill for 20 minutes.
- Set the oven to 180°C.
- Lightly butter a 12 hole tart tray.
- Roll out the pastry on a lightly floured surface. Turn it after each roll so it doesn't stick to the surface.
- Cut out rounds and press into the tart tray.
- Place 2 teaspoons of mincemeat into each hole and brush round the edge with a little yolk.
- Cut out rounds for the top and crimp with your fingers when in place.
- Brush with egg yolk and bake for 20 minutes or until golden and firm.
- Cool in the tray for 5 minutes then transfer to a cooling rack.
- Dust with icing sugar and serve warm.

Paula McIntyre's Down to Earth Cookbook
sweets and treats

Raspberry and hazelnut Madeleines

116

Raspberry and hazelnut Madeleines

Madeleines are shell shaped French pastries. They're brilliant on their own, served straight from the oven, with tea or coffee but also work beautifully as an accompaniment to creamy desserts. Substitute your favourite jam or nut (if you want to avoid the nuts, just add an extra 25g of flour).

INGREDIENT

- 80g butter
- 1 teaspoon honey
- 2 heaped teaspoons raspberry jam
- 2 eggs
- 85g castor sugar
- 80g plain flour
- ½ teaspoon baking powder
- 25g ground hazelnuts

METHOD

- Melt the butter, honey and jam.
- Cool.
- Whisk the eggs and the sugar until pale, fluffy and doubled in volume.
- Sift in the flour and the baking powder
- Add the butter mixture.
- Fold in with the hazelnuts.
- Cover with cling film and chill for 2 hours.
- Set the oven to 180°C.
- Cook for 12–15 minutes or until golden and firm to touch.

Paula McIntyre's Down to Earth Cookbook
sweets and treats

Honeycomb

Honeycomb is the golden, bubbly confection that is the result of the magical addition of baking soda to hot, molten sugar, glucose and honey. Use a fragrant, local Ulster honey for best results.

INGREDIENTS

- 100g castor sugar
- 2 tablespoons water
- 1 tablespoon liquid glucose
- 1 tablespoon local honey
- 1 dessertspoon baking soda, sifted

METHOD

- Place the sugar, water, glucose and honey into a pan and cook on a high heat, without stirring, to a golden amber liquid.
- Carefully add the baking soda, it will bubble up!
- Stir together and pour onto a sheet of parchment paper.
- At this stage allow it to cool as it is for honeycomb or flatten it with a palette knife to make wafers.
- To add a three dimensional aspect to a cake, break the wafers into shards or crumble the honeycomb on top.

Coffee and walnut cake with white chocolate buttercream

Coffee cake transcends both generations and countries. It's as likely to be served in Alabama as it is in Aghadowey. This recipe calls for the baked cake to be doused in a caramel espresso syrup to keep it moist. The buttercream also includes this syrup with the addition of white chocolate, which makes the whole thing quite rich and decadent – if you're going to eat cake you may as well go the whole hog!

Coffee and walnut cake

INGREDIENTS

- 250g soft butter
- 125g castor sugar
- 125g soft brown sugar
- 3 eggs
- 50g chopped walnuts
- 225g self raising flour
- 50g chopped dates mixed with 1 tablespoon espresso powder and 3 tablespoons boiling water
- 1 teaspoon vanilla extract

METHOD

- Set the oven to 180°C.
- Line an 20cm, 8 inch, cake tin with parchment paper.
- Beat the butter and sugars until pale and fluffy – this will take about 10 minutes at full speed with your electric mixer.
- Add the eggs one at a time until incorporated.
- Fold in the flour and date mixture with the vanilla.
- Spoon into the cake tin and bake for about 45 minutes or until an inserted skewer comes out clean.
- Pierce the cake all over with a skewer and spoon over half the caramel coffee syrup.

Paula McIntyre's Down to Earth Cookbook

sweets and treats

Caramel coffee syrup

INGREDIENTS

- 75g castor sugar
- 2 tablespoons water
- 4 teaspoons espresso powder mixed with 100ml boiling water

METHOD

- Place the sugar and water in a non stick pan and heat, without stirring too much, to an amber coloured liquid.
- Carefully add the espresso and cook to a syrup.

White chocolate coffee buttercream

INGREDIENTS

- 110g soft butter
- 250g sifted icing sugar
- 100g chopped white chocolate
- remaining coffee syrup

METHOD

- Gently bring the butter and sugar together in a bowl until the sugar is mixed in.
- Beat with an electric mixer until pale, almost white, and fluffy.
- Melt the chocolate in a heat proof bowl, over a pan of gently simmering water. Ensure the bottom of the bowl and the water don't touch, as it will cause the chocolate to seize.
- Fold the chocolate into the butter mixture with the coffee syrup.
- Spoon into a piping bag and pipe over the cake or just swirl it on top.

Paula McIntyre's Down to Earth Cookbook

sweets and treats

Coffee and walnut cake with white chocolate buttercream

2014

www.rectorshusband.co.uk

CHAPTER SEVEN

Preservation

Picking fruit, vegetables and shoots when they are at the peak of their quality and bottling, jamming or curing them for the leaner months is a tradition that has been carried out for thousands of years. Nowadays, with freezers being taken for granted, there isn't the necessity to do this from a practical, economic point of view. But, adding sugar to summer strawberries, making them into a jam, and bottling them in pretty jars is a much more interesting and delicious way of storing them than just bagging and shoving nature's bounty into the deep freeze.

In turn you'll be provided with flavours that you just can't buy in the shop. When you make your own wine you can experiment and add fruits or vegetables that you have to hand. Blackberries and elderberries are serendipitously ready at the same time and combined together make a rich and fruity wine – the zingy elderberry cutting through the sweet blackberry.

Plus there's the added kick of serving something you've cultivated yourself. The first time I made wine I used the blackberries that teemed from the bushes on the lane at the back of my house. The thrill of presenting homemade wine with the irresistible rocky road (recipe on page 110) made for an unforgettable experience.

Fermentation is the new big thing for restaurant chefs. Last year it was foraging, but just like picking wild fruit and herbs, it's been a practice that's happened for generations. Salting chopped vegetables, adding a few spices and then packing into a jar until they fizz, not only adds a different taste and texture dimension to the original product, but is so good for us, as it replaces the depleting good bacteria in our gut. If you have a glut of vegetables this is an ideal way of preserving them.

Picking something creates a memory that will last a lifetime. When you do it with loved ones, it becomes a still life image in your psyche. Taking what you've harvested and transforming it into wine, pickle or jam will suspend that and replay it every time you see it. I always keep anything I make on proud display – sometimes my kitchen looks like Dr Frankenstein's laboratory but each bottle or jar tells a story and celebrates a place and a special moment in a personal seasonal calendar.

preserves

Sloe and apple jelly

Making jelly from fruit is one of the most rewarding of preservation methods. When you start with a basket of crab apples, bramleys or quinces and capture their magic in an amber hued, viscous liquid, there is very little more rewarding in cooking. Apples and sloes, the fruit of the blackthorn bush, work beautifully together. I gather as many sloes as I can when they're at their best and either make them into this jelly or use them for gin (it's the same method for the damson vodka on page 133).

I use muslin to strain the cooked fruit but I know some people use clean pillow cases to good effect! Like all good things, making jelly takes time but the results are well worth it.

INGREDIENTS

- 750g cooking apples (or use quinces or crab apples instead)
- 750g sloes
- Sugar (550ml of juice will require 700g sugar)

METHOD

- Wash the apples and sloes, remove any blemishes, and place in a preserving pan.
- Add enough water to cover the fruit by half.
- Bring to the boil and simmer until the fruit is soft.
- Strain through muslin and allow to drip for about 12 hours.
- Measure the juice and allow 700g of sugar for every 550ml of juice.
- Place in a preserving pan and bring to a simmer, stirring frequently.
- Place a saucer in the freezer.
- When the sugar has dissolved, bring to a rolling boil for about 10 minutes.
- Take the saucer out of the freezer and drop a little jelly onto it. When the drops set immediately, the jelly is ready.
- Ladle into sterilised jam jars and cool.
- Cover the top with a wax paper disc and seal with a lid.
- Store in a cool, dark place.

Elderberry capers

When the sun eventually pushes through the blanket of winter's grey sky in this country, and the air is filled with the scent of lemony, grassy elderflowers, we're enveloped by the smell of early summer. The lace like, creamy flowers dot the countryside and need to be cherished in their short lived life. The blossom is delicious infused in a sweet cordial but when they give way to green berries, these too need to be nurtured. Salting and pickling them is the best way of seizing their fragrance and keeping it for the winter months.

Ingredients
- green elderberries
- seasalt
- good quality cider vinegar

Method
- When the elderberries are green and hard, pick them in clumps and remove the berries with a fork.
- Wash and pat dry on kitchen paper then cover with seasalt so they are submerged.
- Leave for 3 weeks before washing in cold water.
- Pat dry in kitchen paper again and place in sterilised jars.
- Cover with vinegar, seal and store in the fridge.

Paula McIntyre's Down to Earth Cookbook
preserves

Elderflower cordial

You can buy perfectly good elderflower cordial, but you'd get none of the satisfaction of making it by hand. When you make your own, not only does it have a richer depth of flavour than a generic shop bought variety, but it also provides a story and a sense of place every time you use it.

INGREDIENTS

- 25 elderflower heads, trimmed from the stalks
- 1.5 litres boiling water
- 850g castor sugar
- 2 lemons
- 35g citric acid (found in Asian supermarkets and chemists)

METHOD

- Wash the elderflower heads in cold water.
- Place the sugar in a large, clean bowl or sterilised bucket and pour over the boiling water.
- Stir well and cool.
- Add the lemon slices and citric acid and give it a good stir.
- Add the flowers and cover with a teatowel.
- Leave in a cool place for 24 hours, giving it the odd stir.
- Strain through muslin and pour into sterilised bottles.
- Store in the fridge for up to 3 months.

Paula McIntyre's Down to Earth Cookbook
preserves

Elderflower cordial

Paula McIntyre's Down to Earth Cookbook
preserves

Rose petal syrup

There's a stunning, deep purple rose in my garden called Reine des Violettes. It smells as gorgeous as it looks and making a syrup from the petals is the perfect way of harnessing the scent. The rosey elixir is as good drizzled on summer strawberries and poached rhubarb as it is over roasted Autumn pears or plums. A toot in a glass of sparkling wine on a cold November day will take you back to mid summer for a few intoxicating moments.

INGREDIENTS

- 125g fragrant rose petals (ensure they're from a bush that hasn't been sprayed with pesticides)
- 750g castor sugar
- 350ml water
- 1 lemon, thinly sliced

METHOD

- Wash the rose petals in cold water and pat dry on kitchen paper.
- Place in a bowl with 250g of the sugar and scrunch together to release the scent.
- Cover with cling film and leave overnight, giving it the odd stir.
- Place the remaining 500g of sugar, the water and the lemon in a pan and bring to the boil.
- Simmer until the sugar has dissolved and add the soaked petals and sugar.
- Simmer for 30 minutes or to a syrupy consistency.
- Strain through muslin and pour into sterilised bottles.
- Store in a cool dry place for up to 3 months.

Blackberry wine

When I moved back to the North Coast a couple of years ago I was lucky to live beside a lane lined with healthy blackberry bushes. I'd never made wine before and thought this fruit would be the perfect way of preserving the precious purple pearls for the winter. You'll need a fermenting bucket and demijohn to make wine, plus yeast and pectolase. The whole process takes about a month and after bottling the wine will keep very well in cool place for years. What you'll be left with is a unique flavour, a memory to treasure and a pride borne of using the fruits of your home place as mother nature intended.

INGREDIENTS

- 1.5kg blackberries
- 1kg sugar
- pinch yeast nutrient
- pectolase water

METHOD

- Wash the blackberries and place in a clean fermenting bucket.
- Pour over 4 litres of boiling water and stir frequently until cool.
- Add the pectolase (check the instructions on the packet) and leave for 24 hours.
- Add the yeast and sugar and leave covered for 5 days.
- Strain through muslin into a clean demijohn and top with moist cotton wool.
- When it stops bubbling add an airlock and leave for about 1 month before bottling.

Paula McIntyre's Down to Earth Cookbook
preserves

Whin bush and hibiscus Champagne

When the iconic Giro d'Italia bike race came to Northern Ireland in 2014, I was doing cookery demonstrations at the annual Garden Show Ireland in Antrim Castle Gardens. With everything dyed pink for the weekend, I developed this drink to coincide with the race flashing through the town.

Whin or gorse is the canary yellow flower that grows on hilly ground and has a distinct smell of coconut about it. Hibiscus flowers can be picked up in most delicatessens and add a fragrance and beautiful pink colour to this sparkling drink. Be careful when you add the yeast – a pinch means a pinch. The first time I made this I put in half a teaspoon and when I took the top off the cork, it ended up in a field 250 yards away, narrowly missing an innocent cow!

INGREDIENTS

- 750g castor sugar
- 4 tablespoons dried hibiscus flowers
- 2 pint glasses full of whin bush flowers
- zest and juice of 2 lemons
- 2 tablespoons white wine vinegar
- 4 litres water
- pinch brewers yeast

METHOD

- Mix 4 litres of water and the sugar in a clean fermenting bucket and stir until the sugar dissolves.
- Add the hibiscus and whin flowers.
- Add the lemon zest, juice and vinegar.
- Cover with a teatowel and leave for 2 days.
- Add a pinch of yeast, cover and leave for 5 days.
- Strain through muslin and place in plastic bottles or beer bottles with a ceramic seal top.
- Leave for a week, opening them up now and again so there isn't a gas build up.
- Chill and serve.

Aunt Emily's raspberry jelly

Emily Hampsey is my friend Jane's aunt. She grows raspberries in her garden in the town of Castlerock on the North Coast and then converts them into an amazing raspberry jelly. It's not too sweet and really allows the core flavour of the fruit to shine through. Use late season berries as they have had the benefit of time to allow them to mature into aromatic and intensely rich fruit.

INGREDIENTS

- 1.35kg raspberries (3lb)
- 142ml water (¼ pint)
- juice 1 lemon
- 1.3kg granulated sugar (3¼lb)
- 1 bottle pectin

METHOD

- Place the raspberries and water into a saucepan and simmer for 10–15 minutes.
- Place a sieve over a bucket and line with a double layer of muslin.
- Allow to strain overnight.

- Place a saucer in the freezer.
- Add water to make the liquid up to 1.1 litres or 2 pints.
- Add sugar and lemon juice, and heat slowly until the sugar has dissolved, stirring constantly.
- Bring quickly to the boil and add the pectin.
- Boil rapidly until set is achieved.
- Take the saucer out of the freezer and drop a little jelly onto it. When the drops set immediately, the jelly is ready.
- Pour into sterilised jam jars and cool.
- Cover the top with a wax paper disc and seal with a lid.
- Store in a cool, dark place.

Damson vodka

2014 was a prolific year for damsons and not only did I have my own Aghadowey variety but I was gifted many more along the way. Despite having made gallons of wine, many jars of jam and jellies, the freezer is still bulging. Making damson vodka is a convenient way of using the excess. The damsons are tossed in sugar, placed in a jar with vodka and that's it, apart from giving the jar the odd shake. You can substitute the damsons with other fruit (such as plums, blackberries or sloes) when they're in season and use gin or rum in place of the vodka. The appeal of this method is its sheer simplicity and yet its endless possibilities!

INGREDIENTS

- 1 litre vodka
- 1kg damsons
- 750g sugar

METHOD

- Either prick each damson with a pin several times (life is too short!) or freeze them overnight (a much more practical idea).
- Place them in a sterilised kilner jar, top with the sugar and pour in the vodka.
- Put the lid on and leave in a cool place.
- Every now and then, give the jar a turn or two and a shake.
- After 6 months strain through muslin and bottle.
- You can drink it at this stage but it reaches its best after another 6 months.
- When served with local blue cheese, the fragrant fruitiness in the vodka adds a spicy autumnal note.

Fermented salsa

Fermentation is currently one of those trendy, cheffy things to do but in reality it's been around for centuries. With most of our food today sanitised and pasteurised into oblivion, fermenting food, by adding salt and allowing it to break down, is an easy way of supplementing the 'good bacteria' or probiotics in our diet.

Dearbhla Reynolds is a font of knowledge in this field and runs classes to show how it's done. Her 'Cultured Club' has many converts – me included! Her salsa recipe is a good introduction to this healthy way of eating and if you have a glut of tomatoes, it's an interesting alternative to making chutney. I've experimented with the basic recipe and used grated carrots, beetroot, cucumber and celeriac as an alternative to the tomatoes. Either way it's a fun way of trying out new flavour combinations and perfect for using up leftover vegetables.

INGREDIENTS

- 8–10 ripe tomatoes, chopped
- 1 white onion, peeled and chopped
- 1 chilli pepper, chopped (optional)
- 1 clove garlic, minced
- 2 teaspoons fine seasalt
- ½ teaspoon smoked paprika
- 1 teaspoon toasted cumin seeds
- ¼ teaspoon fresh ground black pepper
- handful fresh coriander chopped

METHOD

- Mix everything together in a clean bowl and squeeze a little to release the juices.
- Transfer to a sterilised kilner jar and place a shot glass on the top.
- Squeeze down.
- Seal the top and leave for 5 days at room temperature – it will fizz a bit.
- Either eat straight away or store in the fridge to enjoy for months.

Paula McIntyre's Down to Earth Cookbook
preserves

Fermented salsa

Paula McIntyre's Down to Earth Cookbook
preserves

Magilligan carrot wine

Paula McIntyre's Down to Earth Cookbook

preserves

Magilligan carrot wine

Mark Stuart, a native of Yorkshire, was a student of mine a few years ago. I quickly discovered that he had a passion for making wine and he's since become my wine making mentor. He produces elixirs from whatever is to hand. His parsley sherries, dandelion wines, rhubarb cider, seabuckthorn gin and a myriad of others are legendary.

This recipe captures the essence of carrots from Magilligan, creating a dry and spicy taste sensation. Like anything worthwhile, good wine takes time, but the result is worth it.

Mark runs wine making classes, check out the rectorshusband.co.uk for details.

INGREDIENTS

- 10kg Magilligan carrots (other varieties can be substituted!)
- 2 very ripe bananas
- 200g chopped sultanas
- 2kg granulated sugar
- 3.5 litres water
- 100ml strong tea
- pinch pectolase
- 25g citric acid
- 1 teaspoon yeast nutrient
- pinch wine yeast
- 1 crushed campden tablet

METHOD

- Wash and peel the carrots, place them in a large pan and cover with the 3.5 litres of water.
- Bring the carrots to the boil and simmer for 20 minutes.
- Carefully strain the carrot water into a sterilised bucket containing sugar, bananas and sultanas.
- When cool, add the tea, pectolase, yeast nutrient and citric acid.
- Stir well.
- Sprinkle on the wine yeast, cover the bucket with cling film and place in a warm place.
- Leave for 7–10 days, stirring daily.
- Strain again to remove the sultanas and bananas, and place in a sterilised demijohn.
- Top up with water.
- Ferment until clear.
- Add a crushed campden tablet and store for 6–12 months.
- Bottle and cork.
- Keep for 6 months before opening.

Pickled wild garlic buds

My sister-in-law Dorothy's parents, Stewart and Eileen, live in Aghadowey. There's a sheugh at the bottom of their garden and come May, it's a green sea of swaying wild garlic. I pick as much as I can and then use it for pesto, pastas and anything else that takes my fancy. I tried to preserve the leaves by pureeing, vacuum packing and freezing them, but sadly they lost their pungency. When the white flowers turn to green buds, around the middle of June, I pick them off with a fork and pickle these perky little shoots. They're as garlicky the next February as they are in early summer! A small amount goes a long way, so a teaspoon of buds will flavour a big pot of pasta very well.

INGREDIENTS

- wild garlic buds
- good quality cider or white wine vinegar

METHOD

- Wash the garlic buds in cold water and pat dry with kitchen paper.
- Remove with a fork and place in sterilised jam jars.
- Cover with vinegar and seal.
- I keep them at the back of the fridge until the new season comes on.

Plum gin

Gin is essentially aromatised raw spirit or vodka. I first got this idea in a restaurant in Birmingham where the young bar man got very animated about all the infusions he'd made that were now proudly displayed on the bar. The bottles were packed with herbs, citrus and spices and cut quite a dash behind the bar. He, like all confident people, was happy to share his basic recipe and I had a lot of fun adding some herbs from the garden and aromatics that I'd gathered from my travels over the years.

INGREDIENTS

- 1 bottle gin (you don't need to go premium here!)
- 4 plums, halved, stoned and sliced
- pared zest of 1 lemon
- 4 cardamom pods
- 4 juniper berries
- 1 slice root ginger
- 1 star anise
- 1 teaspoon dried orange flower blossoms (available online) or pared zest of an orange
- 4 coriander seeds
- 4 peppercorns
- 2 sprigs fresh lavender
- 1 sprig fresh rosemary
- 1 tablespoon honey
- 3 tablespoons sugar

METHOD

- Gently toast the cardamom, star anise, coriander seeds, and peppercorns in a dry pan for about 1 minute – be careful not to burn this, as you just want to release the oils.
- Place the plums in the bottom of a kilner jar, add the toasted spices and remaining ingredients.
- Give it a stir and put on the lid.
- Give it a shake 2 times a day.
- After 5 days, strain and use as you wish. I like it with lots of ice and ginger beer.

Useful food links

Paula McIntyre (paulamcintyre.co.uk) – For further recipes and blogs.

Food NI (nigoodfood.com) – The promotional voice for Northern Ireland's food and drink industry. Its website includes lists of producers, restaurants, events and recipes.

Tourism NI (nitb.com) – For food events happening in Northern Ireland.

Bord Bia (www.bordbia.ie) – For information on products and companies in southern Ireland.

Irish Food Writer's Guild (www.irishfoodwritersguild.ie) – The go to site for food writers in Ireland and I'm proud to be a member.

Slow Food UK (www.slowfood.org.uk) and **Slow Food Ireland** (www.slowfoodireland.com) – These two organisations are part of a global, grassroots movement, with supporters in over 150 countries, which links the pleasure of food with a commitment to the community and the environment.

Livestock and Meat Commission (www.lmcni.com) – For information on beef and lamb.

Ulster Pork and Bacon Forum (www.nipork.com) – The umbrella group for pork farmers in Ulster.

GIY Ireland (www.giyinternational.com) – An organisation that's helping to make food growing the norm.

Seafish (seafish.org) – The authority that supports a profitable, sustainable and socially responsible future for the seafood industry.

Ulster Beekeepers Assocation (www.ubka.org) – All you need to know about local honey.

Index

ale
    slow roast shoulder of lamb with honey and ale brine, and thyme roast carrots, 64

almond
    dollaghan or brown trout almondine, 84–85
    grilled lamb rump steak with mint, chilli and almond butter, 70–71

apple
    apple and cider pudding, 50–51
    apple sponge and homemade cider custard, 46–47
    cider glazed eels with apple and dulse butter, crystallised dulse, and apple and soup celery dressing, 81–83
    duck prosciutto with apple, celery and walnut salad, and blue cheese dressing, 68–69
    sloe and apple jelly, 124

bacon
    cider braised turnip, crispy bacon, 24–25
    Lough Neagh pollan with mealie crushie, 87
    Nora's pot roast cabbage, 23
    pot roast collar of bacon with split peas and parsley, 58
    scallion and potato pancakes with grilled scallions, crispy bacon and creamy parsley dressing, 31–33

bake (see also gratin)
    chicken and broccoli bake, 64
    onions and tomatoes baked with goat's cheese and lovage, 28–29

barbecue sauce
    brisket of beef, Kansas barbecue style, 66–67

beef
    brisket of beef, Kansas barbecue style, 66–67
    daube of beef with beetroot and horseradish, 56–57

beetroot
    daube of beef with beetroot and horseradish, 56–57
    shredded beetroot salad with cumin and ginger, 18–19

biscuit
    Doreen's oat biscuits with whiskey soaked raisins, 106

blackberry
    blackberry and pear crumble, 40
    blackberry wine, 129

blackcurrant
    blackcurrant Barbados cream, 37

black pepper
    smoked salmon fishcakes with horseradish and smoked black pepper dressing, 86
    yoghurt flatbread with gorse flowers and black pepper, 98–99

bread
    89–101
    bread crumbs
    leek gratin with crunchy thyme and soda bread crumbs, 17

bread sauce
    roast chicken, creamy gravy, sausage stuffing balls and Nicola's bread sauce, 60–61

brine
    slow roast shoulder of lamb with honey and ale brine, and thyme roast carrots, 64

brisket
    brisket of beef, Kansas barbecue style, 66–67

broccoli
    chicken and broccoli bake, 64

broth (see soup)

butter
    cider glazed eels with apple and dulse butter, crystallised dulse, and apple and soup celery dressing, 81–83
    grilled lamb rump steak with mint, chilli and almond butter, 70–71
    salted ling brandade with guanciale and smoked local butter, 80

buttercream
    coffee and walnut cake with white chocolate buttercream, 119–121

buttermilk
    buttermilk cake, 112–113
    buttermilk cream with poached rhubarb and lavender shortcake, 41–43

cabbage
    Nora's pot roast cabbage, 23

cake
    buttermilk cake, 112–113
    coffee and walnut cake with white chocolate buttercream, 119–121

capers
    elderberry capers, 125

casserole
    cider braised turnip, crispy bacon, 24–25
    daube of beef with beetroot and horseradish, 56–57
    Nora's pot roast cabbage, 23
    pot roast collar of bacon with split peas and parsley, 58
    slow roast shoulder of lamb with honey and ale brine, and thyme roast carrots, 64

carrot
    Glenarm salmon tarator with roast and pickled carrot salad, 75–77
    gluten free carrot cake with cinnamon icing, 107
    Magilligan carrot wine, 136–137
    paper bag baked carrots with lemon oil, fennel and chilli, and mint labneh, 20–21
    slow roast shoulder of lamb with honey and ale brine, and thyme roast carrots, 64

celery
    duck prosciutto with apple, celery and walnut salad, and blue cheese dressing, 68–69

champagne
    whin bush and hibiscus Champagne, 130

cherry
    rocky road, 110–111

cheese
    duck prosciutto with apple, celery and walnut salad, and blue cheese dressing, 68–69
    onions and tomatoes baked with goat's cheese and lovage, 28–29
    roast pumpkin with ricotta, chilli and mint, 26–27
    soda bread with onions, cheese and scallions, 100

cheesecake
    damson cheesecakes, 48–49

chicken
    chicken and broccoli bake, 64
    chicken broth with potato and soup celery, 62–63
    two roast chickens, three recipes, 59
    roast chicken, creamy gravy, sausage stuffing balls and Nicola's bread sauce, 60–61

chilli
    grilled lamb rump steak with mint, chilli and almond butter, 70–71
    paper bag baked carrots with lemon oil, fennel and chilli, and mint labneh, 20–21
    roast pumpkin with ricotta, chilli and mint, 26–27

chocolate
    chocolate truffles, 108–109
    coffee and walnut cake with white chocolate buttercream, 119–121
    rocky road, 110–111

Christmas
    Christmas pudding, 40

cider
    apple and cider pudding, 50–51
    apple sponge and homemade cider

Paula McIntyre's Down to Earth Cookbook

index

custard, 46–47
cider braised turnip, crispy bacon, 24–25
cider glazed eels with apple and dulse butter, crystallised dulse, and apple and soup celery dressing, 81–83

cinnamon
  gluten free carrot cake with cinnamon icing, 107

clementine
  homemade mincemeat pies, 115

coffee
  coffee and walnut cake with white chocolate buttercream, 119–121

compote
  blackcurrant Barbados cream, 37
  gooseberry shortcake with elderflower (jelly and cream), 51–53

cordial
  elderflower cordial, 126–127

cream
  blackcurrant Barbados cream, 37
  buttermilk cream with poached rhubarb and lavender shortcake, 41–43
  coffee and walnut cake with white chocolate buttercream, 119–121
  gooseberry shortcake with elderflower (jelly and cream), 51–53
  scallion and potato pancakes with grilled scallions, crispy bacon and creamy parsley dressing, 31–33

cumin
  shredded beetroot salad with cumin and ginger, 18–19

custard
  apple sponge and homemade cider custard, 46–47

damson
  damson cheesecakes, 48–49
  damson vodka, 133

dessert
  103–121
  apple and cider pudding, 50–51
  apple sponge and homemade cider custard, 46–47
  Aunt Emily's raspberry jelly, 132
  blackcurrant Barbados cream, 37
  buttermilk cake, 112–113
  chocolate truffles, 108–109
  Christmas pudding, 40
  damson cheesecakes, 48–49
  Doreen's oat biscuits with whiskey soaked raisins, 106
  elderflower poached rhubarb, 114
  gluten free carrot cake with cinnamon icing, 107

gooseberry shortcake with elderflower (jelly and cream), 51–53
homemade mincemeat pies, 115
honeycomb, 118
my Aunt Doreen's Chinese chews, 104–105
pavlova with candied strawberries, raspberries and rose petal syrup, 38–39
raspberry and hazelnut Madeleines, 116–117
rocky road, 110–111
sloe and apple jelly, 124

dollaghan
  dollaghan or brown trout almondine, 84–85

dressing
  cider glazed eels with apple and dulse butter, crystallised dulse, and apple and soup celery dressing, 81–83
  duck prosciutto with apple, celery and walnut salad, and blue cheese dressing, 68–69
  scallion and potato pancakes with grilled scallions, crispy bacon and creamy parsley dressing, 31–33
  smoked salmon fishcakes with horseradish and smoked black pepper dressing, 86

drinks
  blackberry wine, 129
  damson vodka, 133
  elderflower cordial, 126–127
  Magilligan carrot wine, 136–137
  plum gin, 139
  whin bush and hibiscus Champagne, 130

duck
  duck prosciutto with apple, celery and walnut salad, and blue cheese dressing, 68–69

dulse
  cider glazed eels with apple and dulse butter, crystallised dulse, and apple and soup celery dressing, 81–83

eel
  cider glazed eels with apple and dulse butter, crystallised dulse, and apple and soup celery dressing, 81–83

egg
  devilled eggs with smoked salmon, 78–79

elderberry
  elderberry capers, 125

elderflower
  elderflower cordial, 126–127
  elderflower poached rhubarb, 114
  gooseberry shortcake with elderflower (jelly and cream), 51–53

farl
  treacle soda farls, 96–97

fennel
  paper bag baked carrots with lemon oil, fennel and chilli, and mint labneh, 20–21

fish
  73–88

fishcakes
  smoked salmon fishcakes with horseradish and smoked black pepper dressing, 86

flatbread
  yoghurt flatbread with gorse flowers and black pepper, 98–99

garlic
  pickled wild garlic buds, 138

gin
  plum gin, 139

ginger
  shredded beetroot salad with cumin and ginger, 18–19

gluten free
  gluten free carrot cake with cinnamon icing, 107

goat's cheese
  onions and tomatoes baked with goat's cheese and lovage, 28–29

gooseberry
  gooseberry shortcake with elderflower (jelly and cream), 51–53

gorse
  whin bush and hibiscus Champagne, 130
  yoghurt flatbread with gorse flowers and black pepper, 98–99

grape
  walnut bread with salted grapes and rosemary, 92–93

gratin
  leek gratin with crunchy thyme and soda bread crumbs, 17

gravy
  roast chicken, creamy gravy, sausage stuffing balls and Nicola's bread sauce, 60–61

guanciale
  salted ling brandade with guanciale and smoked local butter, 80
  scallion and potato pancakes with grilled scallions, crispy bacon and creamy parsley dressing, 31–33

hazelnut
  raspberry and hazelnut Madeleines, 116–117

hibiscus
  whin bush and hibiscus Champagne, 130

Paula McIntyre's Down to Earth Cookbook

index

honey
- honeycomb, 118
- slow roast shoulder of lamb with honey and ale brine, and thyme roast carrots, 64

honeycomb
- honeycomb, 118

horseradish
- daube of beef with beetroot and horseradish, 56–57
- smoked salmon fishcakes with horseradish and smoked black pepper dressing, 86

icing
- gluten free carrot cake with cinnamon icing, 107

jelly
- Aunt Emily's raspberry jelly, 132
- gooseberry shortcake with elderflower (jelly and cream), 51–53
- sloe and apple jelly, 124

labneh
- paper bag baked carrots with lemon oil, fennel and chilli, and mint labneh, 20–21

lamb
- grilled lamb rump steak with mint, chilli and almond butter, 70–71
- slow roast shoulder of lamb with honey and ale brine, and thyme roast carrots, 64

lavender
- buttermilk cream with poached rhubarb and lavender shortcake, 41–43

leek
- leek gratin with crunchy thyme and soda bread crumbs, 17

lemon
- paper bag baked carrots with lemon oil, fennel and chilli, and mint labneh, 20–21

ling
- salted ling brandade with guanciale and smoked local butter, 80

lovage
- onions and tomatoes baked with goat's cheese and lovage, 28–29

Madeleine
- raspberry and hazelnut Madeleines, 116–117

marshmallow
- rocky road, 110–111

mealie crushie
- Lough Neagh pollan with mealie crushie, 87

mince
- meat and potato pie, 22

mincemeat
- homemade mincemeat pies, 115

mint
- grilled lamb rump steak with mint, chilli and almond butter, 70–71
- paper bag baked carrots with lemon oil, fennel and chilli, and mint labneh, 20–21
- roast pumpkin with ricotta, chilli and mint, 26–27

nut
- coffee and walnut cake with white chocolate buttercream, 119–121
- dollaghan or brown trout almondine, 84–85
- duck prosciutto with apple, celery and walnut salad, and blue cheese dressing, 68–69
- Glenarm salmon tarator with roast and pickled carrot salad, 75–77
- grilled lamb rump steak with mint, chilli and almond butter, 70–71
- my Aunt Doreen's Chinese chews, 104–105
- raspberry and hazelnut Madeleines, 116–117
- rocky road, 110–111
- walnut bread with salted grapes and rosemary, 92–93

oat
- Doreen's oat biscuits with whiskey soaked raisins, 106
- Lough Neagh pollan with mealie crushie, 87
- rousel bread, 94
- wheaten bread, 95

onions
- onions and tomatoes baked with goat's cheese and lovage, 28–29
- soda bread with onions, cheese and scallions, 100

orange
- homemade mincemeat pies, 115

pancake
- pancakes, 90–91
- scallion and potato pancakes with grilled scallions, crispy bacon and creamy parsley dressing, 31–33

parsley
- pot roast collar of bacon with split peas and parsley, 58
- scallion and potato pancakes with grilled scallions, crispy bacon and creamy parsley dressing, 31–33

pastry
- damson cheesecakes, 48
- homemade mincemeat pies, 115

- meat and potato pie, 22

pea
- pot roast collar of bacon with split peas and parsley, 58

pear
- blackberry and pear crumble, 40

pickle
- Glenarm salmon tarator with roast and pickled carrot salad, 75–77
- pickled wild garlic buds, 138

pie
- homemade mincemeat pies, 115
- meat and potato pie, 22

pistachio
- rocky road, 110–111

plum
- plum gin, 139

pollan
- Lough Neagh pollan with mealie crushie, 87

pork
- cider braised turnip, crispy bacon, 24–25
- Lough Neagh pollan with mealie crushie, 87
- Nora's pot roast cabbage, 23
- pot roast collar of bacon with split peas and parsley, 58
- scallion and potato pancakes with grilled scallions, crispy bacon and creamy parsley dressing, 31–33

potato
- chicken broth with potato and soup celery, 62–63
- Dauphinoise potatoes, 30
- meat and potato pie, 22
- rousel bread, 94
- scallion and potato pancakes with grilled scallions, crispy bacon and creamy parsley dressing, 31–33

pot roast (see casserole)

preserves
- 123–139

pretzel
- pretzel rolls, 101

prosciutto
- duck prosciutto with apple, celery and walnut salad, and blue cheese dressing, 68–69

pudding (see dessert)

pumpkin
- roast pumpkin with ricotta, chilli and mint, 26–27

raisin
- Doreen's oat biscuits with whiskey soaked raisins, 106

143

Index

Paula McIntyre's Down to Earth Cookbook

index

rapeseed oil
  gluten free carrot cake with cinnamon icing, 107
raspberry
  Aunt Emily's raspberry jelly, 132
  pavlova with candied strawberries, raspberries and rose petal syrup, 38–39
  raspberry and hazelnut Madeleines, 116–117
ricotta
  roast pumpkin with ricotta, chilli and mint, 26–27
rhubarb
  buttermilk cream with poached rhubarb and lavender shortcake, 41–43
  elderflower poached rhubarb, 114
roast
  Glenarm salmon tarator with roast and pickled carrot salad, 75–77
  roast chicken, creamy gravy, sausage stuffing balls and Nicola's bread sauce, 60–61
  roast pumpkin with ricotta, chilli and mint, 26–27
  slow roast shoulder of lamb with honey and ale brine, and thyme roast carrots, 64
rose petal
  pavlova with candied strawberries, raspberries and rose petal syrup, 38–39
  rose petal syrup, 128
rosemary
  walnut bread with salted grapes and rosemary, 92–93
salad
  duck prosciutto with apple, celery and walnut salad, and blue cheese dressing, 68–69
  Glenarm salmon tarator with roast and pickled carrot salad, 75–77
  shredded beetroot salad with cumin and ginger, 18–19
salmon
  devilled eggs with smoked salmon, 78–79
  Glenarm salmon tarator with roast and pickled carrot salad, 75–77
  smoked salmon fishcakes with horseradish and smoked black pepper dressing, 86
salsa
  fermented salsa, 134–135
sauce
  brisket of beef, Kansas barbecue style, 66–67

roast chicken, creamy gravy, sausage stuffing balls and Nicola's bread sauce, 60–61
sausage
  roast chicken, creamy gravy, sausage stuffing balls and Nicola's bread sauce, 60–61
savoury pancakes
  scallion and potato pancakes with grilled scallions, crispy bacon and creamy parsley dressing, 31–33
scallion
  scallion and potato pancakes with grilled scallions, crispy bacon and creamy parsley dressing, 31–33
  soda bread with onions, cheese and scallions, 100
shortcake
  buttermilk cream with poached rhubarb and lavender shortcake, 41–43
  gooseberry shortcake with elderflower (jelly and cream), 51–53
sloe
  sloe and apple jelly, 124
soda
  leek gratin with crunchy thyme and soda bread crumbs, 17
  soda bread with onions, cheese and scallions, 100
  treacle soda farls, 96–97
soup
  chicken broth with potato and soup celery, 62–63
soup celery
  chicken broth with potato and soup celery, 62–63
  cider glazed eels with apple and dulse butter, crystallised dulse, and apple and soup celery dressing, 81–83
steak
  grilled lamb rump steak with mint, chilli and almond butter, 70–71
stew (see casserole)
strawberry
  pavlova with candied strawberries, raspberries and rose petal syrup, 38–39
stuffing
  roast chicken, creamy gravy, sausage stuffing balls and Nicola's bread sauce, 60–61
syrup
  coffee and walnut cake with white chocolate buttercream, 119–121
  pavlova with candied strawberries, raspberries and rose petal syrup, 38–39

rose petal syrup, 128
thyme
  leek gratin with crunchy thyme and soda bread crumbs, 17
  slow roast shoulder of lamb with honey and ale brine, and thyme roast carrots, 64
tomato
  fermented salsa, 134–135
  onions and tomatoes baked with goat's cheese and lovage, 28–29
traybake
  my Aunt Doreen's Chinese chews, 104–105
  rocky road, 110–111
treacle
  treacle soda farls, 96–97
  wheaten bread, 95
trout
  dollaghan or brown trout almondine, 84–85
turnip
  cider braised turnip, crispy bacon, 24–25
vodka
  damson vodka, 133
walnut
  coffee and walnut cake with white chocolate buttercream, 119–121
  duck prosciutto with apple, celery and walnut salad, and blue cheese dressing, 68–69
  Glenarm salmon tarator with roast and pickled carrot salad, 75–77
  walnut bread with salted grapes and rosemary, 92–93
wheat
  wheaten bread, 95
whin bush (see gorse)
whiskey
  Doreen's oat biscuits with whiskey soaked raisins, 106
Wine
  blackberry wine, 129
  Magilligan carrot wine, 136–137
yoghurt
  Glenarm salmon tarator with roast and pickled carrot salad, 75–77
  paper bag baked carrots with lemon oil, fennel and chilli, and mint labneh, 20–21
  yoghurt flatbread with gorse flowers and black pepper, 98–99